# Harvard Business Review

INTERVIEWS WITH CEOS

## THE HARVARD BUSINESS REVIEW PAPERBACK SERIES

The series is designed to bring today's managers and professionals the fundamental information they need to stay competitive in a fast-moving world. From the preeminent thinkers whose work has defined an entire field to the rising stars who will redefine the way we think about business, here are the leading minds and landmark ideas that have established the *Harvard Business Review* as required reading for ambitious businesspeople in organizations around the globe.

**Other books in the series:**

*Harvard Business Review on Brand Management*
*Harvard Business Review on Breakthrough Thinking*
*Harvard Business Review on Business and the Environment*
*Harvard Business Review on the Business Value of IT*
*Harvard Business Review on Change*
*Harvard Business Review on Corporate Governance*
*Harvard Business Review on Corporate Strategy*
*Harvard Business Review on Crisis Management*
*Harvard Business Review on Effective Communication*
*Harvard Business Review on Entrepreneurship*
*Harvard Business Review on Knowledge Management*
*Harvard Business Review on Leadership*
*Harvard Business Review on Managing High-Tech Industries*
*Harvard Business Review on Managing People*
*Harvard Business Review on Managing Uncertainty*
*Harvard Business Review on Managing the Value Chain*
*Harvard Business Review on Measuring Corporate Performance*
*Harvard Business Review on Negotiation and Conflict Resolution*
*Harvard Business Review on Nonprofits*
*Harvard Business Review on Strategies for Growth*
*Harvard Business Review on Work and Life Balance*

# Harvard Business Review

## INTERVIEWS WITH CEOS

A HARVARD BUSINESS REVIEW PAPERBACK

Printed in the United States of America
04 03 02 01 00 5 4 3 2



The *Harvard Business Review* articles in this collection are available as individual reprints. Discounts apply to quantity purchases. For information and ordering please contact Customer Service, Harvard Business School Publishing, Boston, MA 02163. Telephone: (617) 783-7500 or (800) 988-0886, 8 A.M. to 6 P.M. Eastern Time, Monday through Friday. Fax: (617) 783-7555, 24 hours a day. E-mail: custserv@hbsp.harvard.edu.

**Library of Congress Cataloging-in-Publication Data**
Harvard business review interviews with CEOs.
p. cm. — (The Harvard business review paperback series)
Includes index.
ISBN 1-57851-329-4 (alk. paper)
1. Chief executive officers—Interviews. 2. Industrial management—Case studies. I. Series.
HD38.2.H374 2000
658.4—dc21 99-045196
CIP

*The paper used in this publication meets the requirements of the American National Standard for Permanence of Paper for Publications and Documents in Libraries and Archives Z39.48-1992.*

# Contents

# Harvard Business Review

INTERVIEWS WITH CEOS

# Driving Change

## *An Interview with Ford Motor Company's Jacques Nasser*

SUZY WETLAUFER


## Executive Summary

WHAT HAPPENS WHEN THE WORLD is changing but your organization isn't? And what if that organization has 340,000 employees in 200 countries? In this interview, Jacques Nasser, the new CEO of Ford Motor Company, talks with HBR senior editor Suzy Wetlaufer about these challenges and explains how his company is overcoming them through a unique education program.

Since its very beginnings, says Nasser, Ford has comprised dozens of far-flung divisions and units, each with its own "fiefdom" mind-set. The fiefdoms didn't share information, let alone great ideas. Such behavior stifled creativity and drove up costs.

Today's global environment demands a new and different way of doing business, says Nasser, and to that end, Ford has launched a multifaceted teaching initiative that will reach every one of Ford's employees by year-end. The goal of the program: to help employees view the company in its entirety as shareholders do, and then act that way, too.

At the heart of the initiative is the *teachable point of view,* a five-part written explanation of what a person knows and believes about what it takes to succeed in business. It is more than just a document to be discussed and then filed. It has proven to be a powerful tool for organizational transformation, and not only at Ford. In a commentary accompanying Nasser's interview, Noel Tichy, leadership expert and consultant to Ford, describes the building blocks of the teachable point of view and explores how it can be implemented in any organization determined to change for the better.

---

*Jacques Nasser, the newly appointed CEO of Ford Motor Company, joined Ford Australia in 1968 as a financial analyst. Nasser's family, originally from Lebanon, had long lived in Melbourne, where Nasser spent his teenage years starting businesses, including a bicycle-making operation and a discotheque. His father, an independent businessman himself, watched approvingly as Jacques thrived as an entrepreneur. Little wonder, then, that he greeted his son's decision to join a huge, hierarchical manufacturer with consternation. "Why would you ever want to work for anyone but yourself?" he asked. To him, the excitement of business came from running the works–from being the owner.*

*Today, 31 years after joining Ford, Nasser is asking his employees to see business as his father did–to understand that excitement and success come when* employees think and act as if they own the company. (In fact, they do, to the extent of 20% of the outstanding stock.) Nasser is asking them to adopt, in other words, the capital markets' view of Ford–to look at the company in its entirety, as shareholders do. As Nasser explains in this interview, that's a radically different mentality for Ford. The company has long operated as a collection of fiercely independent fiefdoms united under the flag of their functional or regional expertise. "Ford's fiefdoms don't always war with one another, although that can happen," Nasser says, "but they don't exactly care either about what happens to the domain that contains them all." He recalls a meeting two years ago with 200 of Ford's senior executives. "They all knew everything there was to know about their own divisions," Nasser says. But none could say what the company's assets were. Nor could anyone identify Ford's price-earnings ratio or its economic value added.

Because Bill Ford is leading the board as the company's chairman, Nasser can commit his full attention to leading the company itself. His singular goal as CEO is to replace Ford's fiefdom mind-set with a mentality that will satisfy, if not delight, consumers in the twenty-first century and, in turn, the capital markets. But how do you exact such a transformation–particularly in a company with 340,000 employees across 200 countries? The answer, according to Nasser, is through teaching. As a member of Ford's leadership team, over the past three years he has overseen an intensive, cascading education program that has involved every one of Ford's 55,000 salaried employees. The initiative was launched when the company's most senior leaders were charged with bringing the business case for Ford's transformation to their direct reports. In turn, those direct reports were *charged with becoming teachers and leaders of change by spreading the strategic how and why of Ford's transformation to their direct reports.*

*Ford's change program is based on teaching, but it eschews the traditional classroom setting. Teaching at Ford is achieved through a multifaceted initiative, including small group discussions of strategy and competition, stints of community service, and 360-degree feedback. At the initiative's center is a hands-on, three-day workshop that culminates in an assignment designed to let "students" demonstrate that they understand Ford's new mind-set: within 100 days, they must deliver a significant new cost saving or revenue source to Ford's bottom line.*

*The teaching initiative at Ford has been so effective, Nasser says, that he intends to roll it out to the company's hourly workers this year. "You can't reinvent a company like Ford overnight; we have too much tradition," he explains. "But there is no question that we have to change our fundamental approach to work–we have to change our DNA. And teaching does that better than any other way I know."*

---

***Ford has been making cars for nearly a century. Why change the company's mind-set now?***

If we don't, Ford as we know it won't be around in five years. That's the primary answer, and I would say it's pretty compelling.

No company can survive in a world driven by rapidly changing consumer needs and tastes without having leaders at every level capable of fast decision making. If leaders think and move slowly or operate inefficiently—basically, if they don't keep up with consumers and competitors—then they won't be able to satisfy the capital markets' demand for both profitable growth and unassailable asset utilization. The capital markets are ruthless. They don't care about the stellar performance of one design team, or the financial results of a particular geographic region, or the amazing productivity of one molding plant. The capital markets value the health of a company as a whole. Is the company positioned to meet consumers' needs now and in the future? And can it meet those needs while bringing home great returns on the capital employed?

Another point comes into play here, too. Increasingly, the markets value a global approach to business—an approach in which a company's units, divisions, teams, functions, and regions are all tightly integrated and synchronized across borders. The markets reward the kinds of companies in which, for instance, a manager at an assembly plant in Cologne says, "It would definitely lower my costs to change such-and-such supplier, but it would damage our global strategy for raw material sourcing. I won't do it." When you have a whole company of people thinking like that, you know you're going to see the benefits in overall productivity. And even more important, you're going to see the benefits in innovation, because people will be asking themselves, What can I do to make this whole company work better and smarter and faster? What creative ideas do I have that will really make us grow, not just in my area, but over there, in that division or that one?

***Does that kind of questioning happen at Ford today?***

More and more. But we still have way too much of the fiefdom perspective. I should note, by the way, that I myself used to have that view of our business. When I ran Ford Europe from 1992 to 1994, it was a fiefdom. Every three months or so, we'd get visitors from headquarters who would suggest new ways of thinking about and doing things. And we would wine and dine them and nod at everything they said. Finally, we'd get them on the plane home, and we wouldn't think about a word that they'd said until they came back again. We figured nobody knew more about how to run Ford Europe than we did. We were the experts. We can't do that anymore.

***The transformation effort at Ford, then, is undergirded by two concepts: employees should think like shareholders, and the company as a whole must be able to respond swiftly to—if not anticipate—consumers' needs. Those ideas aren't new. But is this the first time they've been introduced to Ford people?***

We haven't had to introduce these concepts to our people until now. First let me make this clear: the last thing I want to imply is that the new executive team at Ford is a bunch of heroes on white horses, galloping in to save a company in distress. Ford has been in business for 95 years, and you can quibble with its degree of success, but the fact that a company is still around after 95 years is an accomplishment in itself. And when it comes to a global mind-set, Ford is actually ahead of most of its competitors.

But consider the fact that there are legitimate historical reasons Ford evolved into a collection of fiefdoms. Think about Ford's history in three chunks: from its founding in 1905 to the early 1920s, the late 1920s through the 1950s, and the 1960s through the 1980s. The first period was one of colonization for most large U.S. companies—they would send a son off to the U.K., Canada, or Argentina to run a company just like the one back home. The first Henry Ford was an internationalist at heart, I think, because within a very few years of establishing the company here in the United States, he was quickly opening assembly plants all over the world that were essentially smaller versions of the original company in Detroit. Not surprisingly, all the cars looked the same, too; they were all Model T's or Model A's. The competition in this period was basically nonexistent, it was so disorganized.

The next period was one of intense nationalism. All around the world, there was a real sense of national pride. We saw the ugly side with what happened in Germany, but nationalism was on the rise everywhere. Suddenly, there were automotive companies in the U.K., in France, Germany, Australia, and guess what? They were all making their own vehicles. Government policies tended toward nationalist objectives—import quotas, mandatory investments, and the like. Nations wanted to exert their independence and saw the automotive industry as a means of investing in their economies and creating technical skills and employment. The competition during this period tended to be very much national—even the most international competitors operated in large part out of their own regions. The Europeans exported, the Americans exported, and that's how the competitive game was being played.

In the third period, you had the rise of regionalism, with the emergence of the European common market and NAFTA. Countries kept their own political system and social values, but economic trading blocks were being formed. Ford Europe was established in this period. In fact, this was when most of our regional and functional fiefdoms became firmly entrenched. And the system worked very well, given the times and the environment. I would even say the fiefdoms were excellent at what they did: they squeezed every last ounce of efficiency out of the regional model. For instance, back in the period of nationalism, Ford had multiple accounting activities around the world—there were 15 in Europe alone. The regional model got it down to 4—1 in Europe, 1 in the United States, 1 in Asia-Pacific, and 1 in South America. But even with that efficiency, the model doesn't work anymore.

***"The days of looking across town and seeing our major competitors are gone. Now auto companies around the world have ambitions."***

***Because of the globalization of the economy?***

Right. Today we're moving to a fourth stage of economic evolution with the globalization of capital, communications, economic policy, trade policy, human resources, marketing, advertising, brands—you name it. You've got Germans and Japanese producing cars in the United States, and Koreans producing cars in Eastern Europe, and you've got Malaysia exporting cars and parts. Add to that the fact that the automotive industry is now becoming not just a hardware-driven industry but an electronics-driven industry. It's becoming more and more a business that requires huge investments in technology and intellectual capital.

So I don't think there's a choice about globalization anymore. That is, I don't think you can say, "Well, we're just going to remain a national company or a regional company." Some of our competitors are still saying that: "We're quite happy. We're Europeans and we're going to do well in Europe. And yeah, we'll do a little bit in Asia, we'll do a little in South America." That might not be a bad strategy for a short time or for a certain type of company, but for a company of Ford's background and size, I don't think that is a viable alternative.

The days of looking across town and seeing our major competitors are gone. Now auto companies around the world have ambitions, and some of them are world-class players—Toyota and Honda, for example. And we are also going to face competitors with whom we have no experience. So put it all together and you see we are facing an incredible challenge today: more markets open for business, more competitors fighting for dominance, more need for very smart people and fresh ideas. And at the same time, we have to grow. You don't make money by downsizing or shutting plants or reducing your product line. You make money by building the company.

***"We have to change our fundamental approach . . . our DNA. And teaching does that better than any other way I know."***

Ford can't build the company if it holds on to a mindset that doesn't respond swiftly to consumers' needs or pay attention to the capital markets. So that's why we're in the process of reinventing Ford as a global organization with a single strategic focus on consumers and shareholder value. That's not to say you wipe out national cultures or eliminate the idea that it makes sense to have people with expertise in one function or another, but it does mean you strive for some sort of Ford-wide corporate DNA that drives how we do things everywhere. That DNA has a couple of key components: a global mind-set, as I've said, an intuitive knowledge of Ford's customers, a relentless focus on growth, and the strong belief that leaders are teachers.

***Does having a single strategic focus necessarily mean that Ford intends to sell the same products across every market?***

Just the opposite. As a matter of fact, it means that we can actually have products that are tailored to an individual market because we are able to leverage technology and efficiencies around the world. If our cars have common systems that consumers riding in the car don't see or experience—like the front-end crash pulse—then we can put the money and time saved by those common features toward things that consumers do care about in their individual markets. And we can do it faster and cheaper than ever before.

Say we're selling a car in Brazil. It might have the same basic engineering as other Ford cars, but its suspension system will be customized for that country's road conditions, which can be pretty treacherous. At the end of the day, we're capitalizing on our scale, but we're right out front with satisfying our customers.

Some aspects of Ford, however, will be common across markets. For instance, we will have best practices in marketing and employee development. And all major decisions about brand positioning and technology will be made by a central group. Execution, however, will be local, with enough flexibility to ensure that local differences are accounted for. Let me give you an example. In order to have consistent Ford DNA around the world, we need to have consistent policies and practices on compensation. That said, different cultures come at compensation differently—in particular, they have different attitudes about the balance between fixed and variable compensation.

Generally speaking, our long-term goal is to increase the emphasis on variable compensation. In fact, we recently began to roll out a worldwide employee-stock-purchase program to support our drive to have employees think and act as shareholders. But we've gotten some pushback from Ford Australia, mainly because of the tax implications of our program. Given those special circumstances, we agreed that Ford Australia should develop its own stock purchase program. To do otherwise would have been counterproductive—you can't force the world to be the same everywhere.

### *At this moment, how close is Ford to being a global company?*

Let me put it this way: we have a strong international presence. We operate in 200 countries. But having assembly plants in Brazil, product development teams in Germany, and dealerships in Mexico doesn't make us a global company. Look at what happened when we introduced the Ford Escort in Europe in the 1980s. That car, which was intended to be our first global product, was engineered on two continents—North America and Europe. Obviously, that made it impossible for us to capitalize on global sourcing for components. And it was launched individually in every country. Not only did every country come up with its own positioning for the car, but each devised its own advertising message and hired its own advertising agency to get that message across. So you had one car and a substantial number of value propositions. One market was saying, "Yeah, this car's a limousine," and another market was saying it was a sports vehicle. That made it impossible for us to get customers' input into the product after it was out there. Everyone was reacting to a different positioning.

Compare that with the rollout we just had of the Focus, our new compact. It's a great example of where we're headed with our new mind-set. First, the Focus was engineered by one team of engineers. Its concept was launched at one show, in Geneva, and the vehicle itself was launched at one show, in Paris. We brought in journalists from all over the world—1,500 of them. They all drove the Focus on the same roads and in the same conditions. They got the same technological presentation from the same people, and they got the same brand and product positioning delivered to them from the same marketing people. The Focus is a vehicle with a lot of design flair, tremendous spaciousness, great fuel efficiency, and engineering for safety, and we're going to offer it to consumers at an enormous value. That's the way we talk about the car whether it's in Britain, or Canada, or elsewhere. And by the way, we have one advertising agency handling the rollout—one.

***"With the teaching programs we've used over the past three years, our people have delivered $2 billion to our bottom line."***

***Getting from the Escort to the Focus must have required a major cultural shift. How were you able to make that change?***

We realized that the change had to be understood on the individual level. Every manager, every designer, every engineer, every person in the plants had to change his or her way of thinking. And the only way to change at the individual level, I believe, is through teaching. Teaching, we've found, is an amazingly effective way to change an organization. With the teaching programs we've used

## The New Curriculum at Ford

*Ford's teaching initiative comprises approximately a dozen programs. The chart below summarizes four of the most widespread.*

| Program | Participants | Teachers | Components |
|---|---|---|---|
| **Capstone** | 24 senior executives at a time | Jacques Nasser and his leadership team | • Conducted once a year<br>• About 20 days of teaching and discussion<br>• Teams given six months to solve major strategic challenges<br>• 360-degree feedback<br>• Community service |
| **Business Leadership Initiative** | All Ford salaried employees—55,000 to date | The participants' managers | • Three days of teaching and discussion<br>• Teams assigned to 100-day projects<br>• Community service<br>• 360-degree feedback<br>• Participants make videos that contrast the old with the new Ford |
| **Executive Partnering** | Promising young managers—12 so far | Nasser and his leadership team | • Participants spend eight weeks shadowing seven senior executives |
| **Let's Chat About the Business** | Everyone who receives e-mail at Ford—about 100,000 employees | Nasser | • Weekly e-mails describing Ford's new approach to business |

over the past three years, our people have delivered $2 billion to our bottom line, either as increased revenues or decreased costs. And they've delivered them because their mind-sets have changed.

Now, many executives intuitively lead by teaching. In both formal and informal settings, they share their perspectives on strategy and competition, for instance, or they coach individuals to build their skills. I myself taught for years, but I didn't even realize I was teaching. I was talking about the history of Ford, which was the history I grew up with. I told stories about my experiences in different parts of Ford, good and bad. I used those stories as a way of capturing what worked and of describing the pitfalls and opportunities I'd experienced.

This is what's changed: we've systematized teaching as our means of change, made our message consistent, and taken it to a larger audience than ever before. The programs we use are many and varied—Capstone, the Business Leadership Initiative, and Executive Partnering, to name just three. (For an overview of Ford's teaching initiatives, see the chart "The New Curriculum at Ford.") But they all come down to the same thing: people teaching people about the why and how of Ford's new direction. And we create leaders of change in the process.

### *Is teaching the same thing as spreading knowledge?*

Spreading knowledge is part of it. In fact, there is no better, faster way to distribute knowledge around a company than through teaching. In the past 30 years, I have worked for Ford in ten countries. I've faced a military junta in Argentina and a financial meltdown in the Philippines. I've faced hyperinflation, closed markets, open markets, Japanese competition—you name it. I've probably packed 100 years of experience into those 30 years. I could keep all that inside my head, or I could share it with people in the company to help them learn.

### *Beyond "redistributing the wealth" around Ford, what makes teaching an effective tool for change?*

Consider what usually happens in change programs in large companies. A slew of consultants comes in with overheads and Powerpoint presentations. They lecture people about why change is important and how it needs to happen. And when they leave, the people who have sat through the show say, "What do they know? They don't work here." And nothing happens.

But once you start to teach in-house with your own people leading the effort, the teachers themselves have no choice but to behave differently. You've gotten up in front of your people, and you've said, "This is what I believe. This is how we should run the business." After that, it's very hard to disown yourself from the change process. You have to live it and breathe it every day. Teaching enforces the discipline of change.

But I'll tell you something about the discipline of teaching: it is not an easy thing to do. You have to be absolutely committed to it. You can't say, "I'm going to open up the dialogue," and then not really open it up. You have to be genuine in what you are doing. I mean, when you get stopped at the newsstand on a Saturday morning and a factory worker comes up to you and says, "I was thinking about that comment you made in your speech the other week," you can't say, "Well, sorry, it's my free time now. Just send me a note next week." When you open up change—when you bring its case to your people—you have to stay front and center for their questions.

***Wouldn't it be more efficient and just as effective to change the Ford mind-set by moving its people around between fiefdoms?***

It's not enough. People may get a more global point of view with international assignments, but teaching adds something critical. It demystifies why we need to change, why we actually need a global point of view. It demystifies what we're all thinking here at headquarters. You know, you go down a step or two in some parts of this company, and there's a mythology about why we do things the way we do, and the stories don't always match reality. As a result, a wall builds up between senior management and the people who execute the strategy. The people on the front lines end up saying, "They want change up there," and they don't know why, and they don't care.

Teaching allows you to replace the old mythology with a new and better one. When I first came to Dearborn, I decided to invite people to take a look around my office and answer any questions they had. We had thousands of people through. And you know what they asked? "Where's the Jacuzzi?" A story had started—I don't know where, and I don't know how—that when I came to Dearborn, I had an elaborate office designed for myself with a health club and a Jacuzzi in it. So people came, and they saw that there was no Jacuzzi. That was part of breaking the old mythology, which was that the senior executives were so disconnected from the real work of this company that they were spending their afternoons in Jacuzzis.

With teaching, we've been able to introduce new stories, to create a different folklore about what's possible at Ford. That's how you build a new culture—through stories. I tell a lot of stories that have the same moral—that working at Ford does not have to be about working in a single area. It can be about working and caring for the whole company.

One of my favorite stories involves our consumer research department here in Dearborn. A while back, they got it in their heads that maybe we should change the look of the front grille on the Explorer. They asked me about it, and I said no, but they were bound and determined. So one weekend, they got 100 paid people in here—probably provided by some focus-group company—and they had them walk around and look at 15 different grilles, each person holding a little clipboard, jotting down impressions. I don't know exactly what it cost, but it was too much. And I'll tell you why. If we don't know intuitively the look that Ford customers want and expect from us, then we're dead. When it was all over, the focus group participants picked the Explorer grille. Of course they did—that grille is the Ford look at its essence and we can't go wasting time and money messing with that. There are bigger and more important battles out there. I tell this story because it demonstrates the absolute need to understand the essence of brand and consumers.

***Have you changed your stories since you started the teaching initiative at Ford?***

Definitely, because you learn what works. You learn what your people know. For instance, a few years ago, I started meeting with small groups of senior executives to talk about shareholder value and what that means in the daily approach to our jobs. The first few times, I spent hours talking about financial ratios. But it wasn't until someone was brave enough to come up to me afterward and say, "What's a P/E ratio?" that I realized why so few people in the company were thinking about shareholder value. They didn't understand it as a concept. The same with growth. No one understood why we had to grow. The topic was talked about only by a few guys up in finance. Even senior executives, most of whom had grown up within a single function, had little understanding of what drove shareholder value and how to measure and track our total company performance in the manner of the capital markets.

***Let's talk about some of the components of the teaching initiative at Ford. Which one would you say is the most effective?***

You can't deconstruct the components. No single component is more powerful than another—they reinforce one another. And they all build off the same foundation: *the teachable point of view*, which is a document written by people to explain their theories about competition and success, and also has the powerful effect of turning everyone in the organization into a leader and teacher of change. (For a discussion of the teachable point of view, see "The Teachable Point of View: A Primer" at the end of this article.)

Our first teaching program was called Capstone. It was launched in 1996 as a means for both Alex Trotman, then CEO and chairman, and his senior team to share their teachable points of view and to develop leaders from the top several hundred executives in the company. Capstone continues today.

### *How does Capstone work?*

First, my leadership team and I select four strategic challenges facing Ford. For instance, one challenge was to figure out what our distribution channels should look like given the rise of the Internet and the emergence of large retail outlets—these superstores for cars that are popping up. Each one of these challenges is then assigned to a team of six senior executives from around the world. They've got six months to tackle it, with one member of the leadership team along for the ride as a sponsor, guide, and coach.

The teams begin the six-month process with an intensive five-day workshop. A lot goes on. My team and I share our teachable points of view. We have team-building exercises, community service projects, 360-degree feedback, coaching, and plenty of conversation and debate about the projects that lie ahead.

The workshop concludes with a long dialogue between me and the participants, along with their spouses or partners. And I mean it when I say long; these conversations can last up to three or four hours. Spouses and partners are included because I don't think you can effect change in a company without acknowledging that the kind of transformation we're talking about is going to influence people at home as well as on the job. I don't give a speech. We talk about how global careers affect families; we share ideas about ways to fix the company; we talk about the exciting new business opportunities that exist for Ford. Sometimes these sessions get pretty intense, which is great. That intensity is energizing. And when it's all over, the Capstone participants are asked to create their own teachable points of view.

Following the workshop, the senior executives go back to their day jobs. Their Capstone projects will take up about 30% of their time over the next six months. The teams are global, so working together can be pretty challenging. They have to figure out ways to meet face-to-face, how best to use e-mail, and when to use videoconferencing and teleconferencing. Halfway through the project, all the participants meet for a coaching and check-in workshop. The teachers are members of my top team or previous Capstone participants. There's the whole idea of leaders teaching and leaders developing leaders.

The final session of Capstone lasts several days, and again it's all about teaching. My top team and I review recommendations from each team and decide what to implement. Every participant receives extensive feedback on his or her performance from fellow participants as well as from the top team.

Capstone is about learning, but its results have been anything but academic. Take that matter of distribution channels that I mentioned. In their six-month block, the team members studying it got out in the field, benchmarked Ford against other consumer companies, and spent time with our dealers. Based on their analysis, they decided we should adopt a whole new strategy—basically, they recommended we start acquiring dealerships in different regions and create our own superstores with our dealers as business partners. They developed a business model for their plan, came up with an implementation process, presented the idea to the board, and sold it to senior management—all with incredible speed. Within weeks of their presentation, we launched their

***"Our company now has more than 1,500 leader-teachers worldwide who have reached a total of 55,000 salaried employees."***

approach, and today it is a critical part of our long-term strategy.

***Let's talk about Ford's Business Leadership Initiative.***

BLI brings teaching to a larger audience. It began when the top 200 executives at Ford were trained as teachers in a three-day workshop so that they could take their own teams off for three days and teach them about Ford's new approach to business. These teachers were also shown how to design 100-day projects for teams of BLI participants—projects that tackle cost problems or discover new sources of revenue in their own areas. By the end of 1997, we had completed 200 BLI workshop series involving about 20,000 of our salaried people. Today BLI has spread throughout the organization to the extent that our company now has more than 1,500 leader-teachers worldwide who have reached a total of 55,000 salaried employees.

Again, like Capstone, the BLI projects are an incredibly important part of the learning process. And even though they're smaller than the strategic challenges taken on by the Capstone participants, they certainly aren't little, make-work assignments. Teams have to show they have made a positive impact on shareholder value, be it through cutting costs or enhancing growth or improving customer satisfaction. For instance, one team had the objective of increasing sales of accessories that are offered on light trucks, such as the Expedition and the Navigator. The project had a revenue target of $18 million and a profit target of $4.9 million. In another BLI session, eight teams got together and decided to establish a center within Ford to double the productivity and halve the time of IT systems development. Their target for profit effect was $40 million. It looks as if both of those projects will achieve their goals by the end of 1999.

***In Capstone, the concept of shareholder value is central to the curriculum. Is the same true for BLI?***

Definitely. At the outset, a lot of our people didn't know Ford's market capitalization, or its price-earnings ratio, or why either of those things mattered. We basically had to introduce the concept of capital markets. We had to talk to people about where Ford really sat competitively: how we looked compared to General Motors—and compared to Microsoft, General Electric, and Wal-Mart. People are thrilled to learn this information, believe it or not. They want to put their daily work into a bigger economic context.

***Every BLI participant spends at least half a day in a community service project. Why?***

There are a couple of objectives. First, one of Ford's strategies is to be a world-class corporate citizen. That means far more than contributing dollars to society; it means we must actively contribute our time and energy to the communities in which we operate. Second, working in a community is a very powerful leadership-development experience. Ford people have built schools in Mexico, worked with the homeless in New York, and cared for the elderly in Hong Kong. Our people have worked side by side with community activists who have shown what it takes to get things done under the most daunting circumstances.

One organization that teaches our people a lot is Focus: HOPE in Detroit. It distributes food to about 80,000 people a month and trains thousands of young people in all sorts of life and job skills. It has trained almost 1,500 machinists, for example. The experiences at Focus: HOPE have fundamentally changed many of our people. One Ford executive who worked there told me he would never complain again about the limits of his budget. He said the experience showed him what we meant when we talked about working against the odds.

After the community service portion of BLI is over, we bus everyone back to the training center and we talk about leadership. We also talk about the emotions of change. Those emotions can be brutal—we get them out, we let people air them. And then we give them a final assignment. We say, "Here's a video camera. You have 45 minutes to plan, script, and shoot a five-minute movie that compares the new and old way of doing things at Ford. By the way, the best movie—which you will judge yourselves—will be shown on the third day of the workshop when Jac or one person from the senior team will be with you."

***Can you describe some of the winners?***

There was a hilarious one not too long ago. For the old Ford way, they showed a bunch of people standing around a swimming pool. They were all wearing suits. And then one of them falls in, and he clearly can't swim. He's screaming and flailing all over the place. All the people on the side of the pool start to wring their hands—you know, they're fretting. They're saying, "God, we've got a problem. We've got to call McKinsey. Maybe we should put a committee together." And the guy in the pool, of course, drowns.

In the video depicting the new Ford, the guy falls into the pool, and everyone jumps in to save him. It was funny, but underneath there are some deep themes about the great stuff that happens when you get rid of bureaucratic behavior.

***Do people ever complain that the video exercise is silly? That is, are people cynical about the Capstone or BLI programs? After all, it's something of a forced march.***

Not really. People are energized by the learning process. I'm not saying Capstone and BLI are easy, and I'm certainly not going to tell you that change is easy. People are out of their comfort zone. In fact, for many in the BLI program, the workshop is the hardest three days they've ever had on the job. But there's something exhilarating about accepting change—especially about understanding that you can be a positive part of it. Change doesn't have to push you along; you can ride along with it.

***Executive Partnering is another component of the teaching initiative at Ford. What does it involve?***

Executive Partnering targets young managers with leadership potential. We assign these people to seven top executives over eight weeks. In that period, the young managers basically shadow their partners. They travel with them and attend dinners, teaching sessions, meetings with clients and customers. They are exposed to the full range of business challenges that leaders grapple with every day—the inevitable paradoxes of leadership, resource allocation issues, the conflict between urgent matters and long-term goals.

We arrange the program so that three young managers are partnering at the same time. In addition to their individual experiences, they are also asked to work together on an immediate business problem. That builds their collaborative skills and gives them some cross-functional experience in a compressed time frame.

Executive Partnering has been one of our most effective development activities ever, based on the feedback from both sides of the equation. In fact, it has been so well received that we're extending it to other levels of the company.

***Another part of the teaching initiative is your "Let's Chat About the Business" e-mails. How often do you send those out, and who receives them?***

They go out every Friday at 5 P.M. to about 100,000 employees—basically everyone who receives e-mail in the company. They're just another way to share as much information—unfiltered—as broadly as possible throughout the company and to encourage dialogue at all levels. They're also a chance for me to describe what's happening in the company from the capital markets' perspective. I talk very explicitly about our stock price and shareholder value. I quote what Wall Street auto analysts are saying about Ford stock—buy, sell, or hold. I talk about what our competitors are doing. For instance, I gave my opinions about the meaning of the merger between Chrysler and Daimler-Benz. I also describe what's happening in the global economy. Last year, for instance, I used a "Let's Chat" e-mail to state my case for the changing paradigm in the automotive battleground.

One of the best aspects of the "Let's Chat" e-mails is how many responses I get. People take me on. They ask questions. They make suggestions about how we can do better. They push my thinking. That's what teaching is all about.

***You seem convinced that the teaching effort at Ford will be successful in changing the company's mind-set and its performance. Why?***

I know some people are great actors, but I've seen a tremendous change in how people view the business. It's more subtle than a change in our culture, although that's happening. The shift involves the way people are thinking about their careers and contributions within the company and how they're thinking about the competition.

I've seen the company's mind-set change before. When I was in Australia, I saw people fundamentally change the way they work.

***You were appointed president of Ford Australia in 1990, after 17 years of working for Ford in other parts of the world, but it wasn't much of a homecoming, was it?***

It was a disaster. Ford Australia was basically the same as Ford worldwide, except that it had 15,000 people instead of 340,000. It was a very function-driven company, to the point where none of the divisions talked to one another. I mean, no one ever said, "Hey, let's get together for the good of the business." But Australia was a protected environment and so, even with the infighting, the company had fared pretty well. Then the market opened up, and all of a sudden you had competition from everywhere—Japan, Europe, Korea.

The first thing that happened was that market share tanked, and then it started to lose money, and then quality went bad, and things started to fall apart. The government didn't trust the company, and the unions didn't trust management, and the press turned against the brand. Employee morale was terrible. The situation was so serious that some people within Ford's higher levels thought there really was no solution and, even more than that, that saving Australia wasn't worth it.

I wasn't prepared to accept those ideas because I remembered Ford Australia as it had been. True, the environment had changed, but there was still a core of really dedicated, good people. They just had to start relating to one another.

*Did you use teaching?*

We didn't call it that then, but it was teaching—helping people understand the business case for collaboration. I was up in front of the people constantly saying, "This is where we are going, why we are going there, and how we're going to get there." For two or three years, all we did was teach.

*What happened?*

People learned, and the company turned around. We became leaders in quality. With the unions, it went from a situation where their leadership wouldn't talk to us to what was a model relationship based on honesty and trust. And a feeling grew within the company that we were winners—and we were. We started launching vehicles on time and under budget, and we started making money.

Much of what I learned in Australia I'm now applying to Ford worldwide, and already I can see the same kind of transformation taking place. But I also have no doubt that there's no end. Three years from now, we still won't be there. But I'll tell you something: because of teaching, the Ford you see today has no resemblance to the Ford of five years ago. If you dissected us and inspected every blood vessel, we're different; our DNA has changed. I don't think we'll go back.

---

## The Teachable Point of View: A Primer

### *by Noel Tichy*

THREE THINGS CAN BE SAID about change in today's intense competitive environment: it's hard, it's necessary, and most people are bound to resist it. The question for leaders, then, is, what actually makes change happen? As Jacques Nasser has found at Ford, the answer is teaching. Or more specifically, teaching based on a mechanism I call the *teachable point of view*, which turns leaders into teachers and their students into teachers and leaders, and so on. I did not invent the teachable point of view. I recognized it and gave it a name. Great leaders—be they of corporations, churches, or armies—have probably been using it forever. Today, in fact, it is galvanizing change programs not only at Ford but also at General Electric, AlliedSignal, PepsiCo, and hundreds of other organizations large and small.

The teachable point of view, simply put, is a written explanation of what a person knows and believes about what it takes to succeed in his or her own business as well as in business generally. What do consumers really value? What would it take to knock out the competition? What dynamics—from on-line buying to demographic changes—will drive the markets in five years? What kind of people should the company hire in order to reach its goals? How does a leader know when to dive into a new technology? How does he or she know when to abandon a sinking ship?

The teachable point of view is not, however, just a how-to manual. It is a *why* manual as well. (I'm using the word "manual" loosely here—most teachable points of view can fit on two pages.) It identifies why a person approaches work as he or she does; it opens up his or her assumptions, beliefs, and experiences to colleagues, bosses, and subordinates. I often think of the teachable point of view as the antidote to the "black box" in people's heads—the box that conceals the origins of good ideas and important insights.

Sometimes I'm asked who should create a teachable point of view within a company, even a small one. The short answer is everyone. But the sequence in which these documents are written is important. First, the leaders need to get theirs done, and those documents need to be discussed, debated, and ultimately aligned. This process takes time and intensive work; at Ford, Nasser and his team created their teachable points of view during four off-site meetings over a four-month period.

Then the teaching begins. The leaders should share their teachable points of view with the next level of executives, and after debate and discussion, those people should write their own teachable points of view. Next, that group—now leader-teachers themselves—should share their teachable points of view with their reports. And the teaching goes on and on.

All teachable points of view look a bit different; some are long and filled with charts and graphs. Others are handwritten letters. But they all, in my experience, include four basic building blocks: ideas, values, emotional energy, and edge.

The ideas section lays out a person's theory about organizational success in terms of products or services, distribution channels, customer segments, and the like. It states the set of assumptions and beliefs the person holds about what will make a company profitable in the marketplace. At GE, for example, Jack Welch's teachable point of view uses the idea section to describe a world driven by deflationary pressures. In such an environment, GE cannot only "love to make great things in factories and send them out the door in a box." Going forward, the company will thrive only if it operates as a service company that also makes high-quality products. GE is on its way to realizing that vision; today it derives at least two-thirds of its revenue from services worldwide.

The values section of the teachable point of view can encompass an individual's personal ideology—such as a strong belief in honesty and integrity—but it must also explain the values he or she endorses in supporting business goals. Take Jack Welch again. His vision for GE requires that the company reach its markets quickly (how else does a service company succeed?) and that its people share best practices across divisions. For those reasons, he coined the value of "boundarylessness," which means, in his words, "behavior that is open, where people act without regard to status or functional loyalty and also look for ideas from anywhere."

Third, the teachable point of view contains a person's thinking about how to motivate other people. Some leaders believe that face-to-face coaching works best; others favor formal development programs, task forces, and the day-to-day mechanisms of strategy formulation, budgeting, and performance reviews. The action-learning programs Nasser describes in the interview, such as Capstone, BLI, and Executive Partnering, demonstrate his theory about motivation: People are energized when they understand the competitive context of their work. And they are further motivated when they are expected to deliver results. Nasser believes in the power of scale and speed: Energy is contagious. The faster and wider you roll out an initiative, the more the electricity spreads.

Edge refers to a person's individual thought process for making difficult decisions–the yes or no decisions. How do you make the tough calls? If an emergency room triage nurse were to explain her edge, for instance, she would describe what factors help her prioritize patient care: her medical knowledge, experience, and values. Everyone "knows" that a person with a gunshot wound must be treated before a person with a toothache. Similarly, everyone "knows" that an unethical employee should be fired. The discussion of edge in a teachable point of view, however, makes the why and how of these decisions clear.

There are three main reasons the teachable point of view works so well in change situations. First, the very act of creating and testing a teachable point of view makes people better leaders. As they step back from the day-to-day ferment of business and reflect on what they know, leaders come to understand why they lead as they do–why they make certain decisions about competitive threats, for instance, or why they act in certain ways in crisis situations. In the process, leaders penetrate their underlying assumptions about themselves, their organizations, and business in general. Implicit knowledge becomes explicit and can then be questioned, refined, and honed to both the leader's and the organization's benefit.

Second, the power of the teachable point of view is in its multiplier effect and its speed. Once Nasser had articulated his teachable point of view, he taught it to 200 other leaders, who taught it to 1,200 more, who taught it to 55,000 more–all within a year. The same phenomenon could be seen at PepsiCo, as CEO Roger Enrico passed on his teachable point of view to 110 executives, who in turn passed it along to 20,000 people in 18 months. At AlliedSignal, CEO Larry Bossidy used the teachable point of view to reach all 86,000 of the company's employees in one year.

Third and finally, the teachable point of view also expedites one of the leader's most difficult and mission-critical tasks: developing people. Typically, leaders develop other leaders by example. That can take a long time and leaves many insights unarticulated. The power of the teachable point of view is that it gives leaders an explicit body of knowledge to impart. It helps them construct a framework for their own ideas, which helps others build knowledge as well.

**Noel Tichy** *is a professor of organizational behavior and human resource management at the University of Michigan Business School in Ann Arbor. He is the coauthor, with Eli Cohen, of* The Leadership Engine *(HarperBusiness, 1997). He has been consulting for Ford on its teaching initiative for the last two years.*

**Originally published in March–April 1999**
**Reprint 99211**

# Organizing for Empowerment

## *An Interview with AES's Roger Sant and Dennis Bakke*

SUZY WETLAUFER

### Executive Summary

THE TOPIC OF EMPOWERMENT is receiving a lot of attention, but how many employees are truly empowered? At the global electricity giant AES Corporation, the answer is all 40,000 of them.

In this interview, chairman Roger Sant and CEO Dennis Bakke reflect on their trials and triumphs in creating an exceptional company and explain how their employee-run company works.

When they founded AES in 1981, Sant and Bakke set out to create a company where people could have engaging experiences on a daily basis–a company that embodied the principles of fairness, integrity, social responsibility, and fun. Putting those principles into action has created something unique–an ecosystem of real empowerment.

What does that system look like? Rather than having a traditional hierarchical chain of command, AES is organized around small teams that are responsible for operations and maintenance. Moreover, AES has eliminated functional departments; there's no corporate marketing division or human resources department. For the system to work, every person must become a well-rounded generalist–a mini-CEO. That, in turn, redefines the jobs of the people at headquarters. Instead of setting strategy and making the "the big decisions," Sant and Bakke act as advisers, guardians of the principles, accountability officers, and chief encouragers.

Can other companies successfully adopt the mechanics of such a system? Not unless they first adopt the shared principles that have guided AES since its inception. "Empowerment without values isn't empowerment," says Sant. "It's just technique," adds Bakke.

---

*Few management topics have received as much attention recently as empowerment. In the past four years alone, nearly 30,000 articles about empowerment have appeared in a wide variety of print media, from the* Wall Street Journal *to* Nation's Restaurant News. *By and large, the press is positive: executives and factory workers alike have extolled the virtues of organizations in which frontline employees are charged with the authority to make and execute important decisions without top-down interference. Empowered organizations are said to be hothouses of autonomy and trust, where people at all levels take full responsibility for their work and for the organization's performance.*

*But there are skeptics. Management expert Chris Argyris, for instance, recently argued that most talk of empowerment is lip service. (See "Empowerment: The Emperor's New Clothes," HBR May–June 1998.) Many executives claim that they are empowering their employees, Argyris says, but employees know better. They are still either second-guessed or left out in the cold on big decisions. Indeed, Argyris goes on, the gap between empowerment's myth and its reality is one reason that employees are so cynical these days. Empowerment is a false promise, nothing more.*

*In the middle of this debate are executives who consider empowerment a sound business idea–or even a noble cause–but are perplexed about how to make it work. They are struggling with empowerment's mechanics. What kind of hiring practices results in frontline employees with the knowledge and the skills required to make critical business decisions? In a truly empowered organization, what controls should exist, if any? If authority is extended to the far reaches of an empowered organization, what is left for the leaders to do?*

*AES Corporation, the global electricity company based in Arlington, Virginia, has been refining those mechanics for years. Founded in 1981 by Chairman Roger Sant and CEO Dennis Bakke, the company today operates roughly 90 electricity plants in 13 countries, employing some 40,000 people. (For a look at AES's performance from 1990 through 1998, see the exhibit "AES: Growing Up and Growing Fast.") In this interview with HBR senior editor Suzy Wetlaufer, the two executives discuss the company they have built–both in terms of its day-to-day logistics and its philosophical foundations.*

***Did you set out to make AES a "poster company" for empowerment?***

**Bakke:** We knew that we wanted to create a very different kind of company, that's for sure. I don't think we used the word *empowerment*—I'm not sure it was even around in 1981.

Our main goal at the beginning was to build a company that we ourselves would want to work in. The actual type of business wasn't really important, to tell you the truth. It could have been an energy conservation company; it could have been steel. It ended up being an electricity company. We just wanted to create a company that embodied the four principles that we felt mattered in any kind of community, be it a business, church, village, or whatever: fairness, integrity, social responsibility, and fun.

That last one—fun—is very important. Some companies just tag it on to the end of their mission statements. But for us, fun is really central. We never set out to be the most efficient or most powerful or richest company in the world—only the most fun. And I think we're getting there.

**Sant:** I would agree. But the word *fun* can be misleading. We're not talking about having parties all the time. That's not why AES is fun. It's fun because the people who work here are fully engaged. They have total responsibility for decisions. They are accountable for results. What they do every day matters to the company, and it matters to the communities we operate in. We do celebrate a lot—because lots of great things are happening. We just did a billion-dollar deal, for instance, and that called for a party. But it's what happens before the celebrations that's really fun.

**Bakke:** The struggle before the deal, for instance, the challenge and the creativity required to make it work, taking risks, even the sleepless nights. Believe it or not, those things really are fun because they engage people—heart, mind, and soul. And that was the kind of company we set out to create, one in which people could have engaging experiences on a daily basis.

***What goes on within AES that makes those experiences possible?***

**Bakke:** It has to do with our structure and our practices—hiring, compensation, information flow, and so on. They're like an ecosystem. Everything about how we organize gives people the power and the responsibility to make important decisions, to engage with their work as businesspeople, not as cogs in a machine.

I'll give you an example. We have a team member in India; he's been with us for three years. He and his team wanted to buy two coal plants. Most board members, including me, were very interested in getting those plants, and we urged him to bid $170 million. He said no, primarily based on strong advice he got from his colleagues around the company. The returns weren't good enough, he believed; there was too much risk. He bid $143 million—and he won. The important point is this: even with advice from the most senior people in the company, the decision belonged to him. We let him make it, and he made it. The AES system is designed to make sure power gets distributed throughout the organization.

**Sant:** Our system starts with a lack of hierarchy. We abhor layers. We avoid them like the plague. The more authority figures you have above you, the more likely it is

## *AES: Growing Up and Growing Fast*

*AES is the world's largest global power company, and its revenues, profits, and generation capacity show no signs of slowing.*

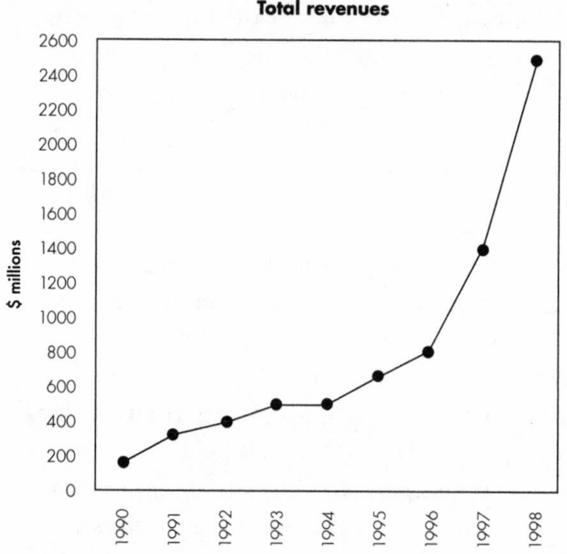


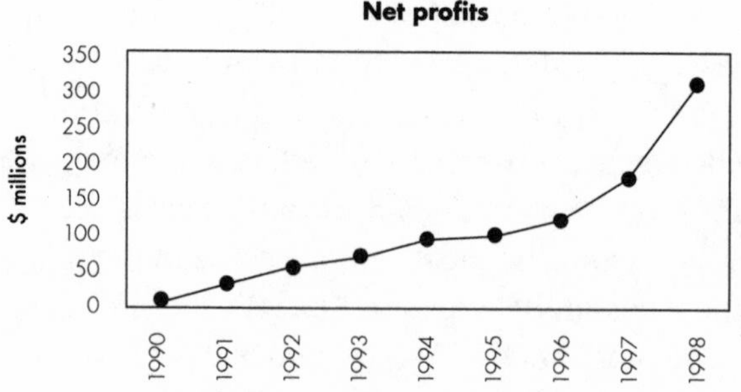


Source for 1998 estimates: Lehman Brothers

## Net generation capacity

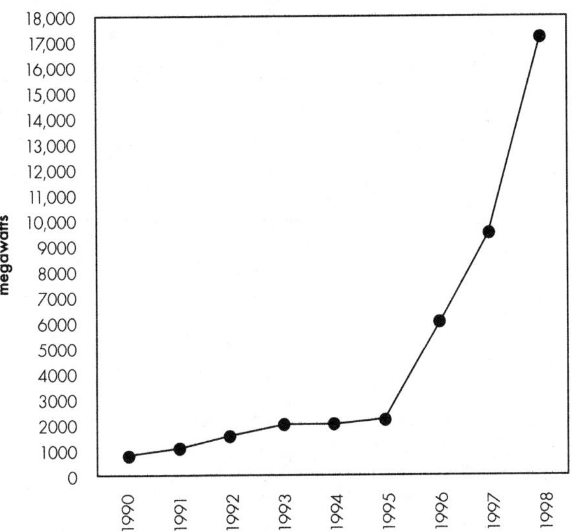


## AES at a glance

**Mission:**
to help serve the world's need for electricity

**Goal:**
to be the leading global power company

**Guiding principles:**
fairness, integrity, social responsibility, and fun

Source for 1998 estimate: BT Alex. Brown Incorporated

that you won't make decisions yourself. So we organize around small teams. The plants and business development activities are grouped into 11 regions; each one led by a manager. Every plant has a manager as well. He or she oversees 5 to 20 teams within the plant, each containing about 5 to 20 people, including a team leader.

**Bakke:** So for instance, there's a team that oversees the control room and one that oversees everything having to do with the fuel for the plant. There's almost always a water treatment team. All our plants clean water in order to power the facilities. They take rainwater or effluent from the city treatment facility, or water from a river or a well, and they make it very clean. Purer, even, than drinking water, because if any minerals or dirt are present, they will contaminate the blades and tubes of the turbine and boiler and cause major problems for the equipment.

**Sant:** We're moving toward a system in which each team has total responsibility for its area both in terms of operations *and* maintenance. That's different from most of the industrial world, where the two are kept separate. Most industrial settings have a special maintenance group that comes and fixes things when they break and tries to keep things running efficiently. But we want people to take ownership of the whole—the way you care about your house. You run it; you keep it up; you fix it. When something goes wrong, you own the problem from start to finish. And nobody has to tell you to do it because the responsibility is all yours—operating and maintaining.

**Bakke:** We have very few layers, and teams take full responsibility for their work. But what always seems to surprise people most about us is that we don't have any staff to speak of; we have tried to eliminate all groups of functional specialists. We don't have a corporate marketing division or a finance group or an environmental compliance division. And we certainly don't have a human resources department—we don't even allow people to use those words to describe our people: *human resources*. That's not what they are—assets like fuel or money. People are special and unique. So the only staff we have now—and that's because we haven't figured out how to push this activity to local teams—is an accounting group. It includes about 25 people at the corporate office. They collect financial information from around the company so it can be reported to the public. This is a bigger group than we would like, but it's not too bad for a company with a market capitalization of around $9 billion.

**Sant:** We also work incredibly hard to make sure that operating teams don't contain more than one of each kind of expert or specialist.

**Bakke:** I joke that one engineer is great, but two together is a disaster. And you can say the same thing about lawyers or any other type of specialist. As soon as you start to cluster them, all sorts of bad things happen. Mainly, corporate learning slows down enormously because the experts tend to talk and listen to one another, both inside and outside the company.

**Sant:** For the system to work, every person in the company has to become a well-rounded generalist who understands all aspects of our operation, who understands the economy in which we work, and who has the good of the whole company in mind when he or she makes decisions. It's like every AES person is a mini-CEO.

### *How does that CEO perspective get formed?*

**Bakke:** There are lots of ways we aim for that goal. One is job rotation. People move from team to team and from plant to plant. The example of Pete Norgeot's career with us is a good case in point. Before joining our Thames plant in Connecticut, he was a heavy-machine operator. His first assignment with us was as a member of the fuel-handling team. He stayed with that team for six months, then shifted to the water treatment team, and then to the boiler team. For three years, he basically went from group to group. He studied all the technical books he could—we have manuals on every aspect of our operation, and you can use them to help prepare for the qualification exams that you must pass before you can work in an area. After spending three years at Thames, he learned of an opportunity in our Medway plant in England, and he took it. After a few years, he was selected to be the plant manager at our new Barry facility in Wales.

***"We try to reinvent the wheel every time we get a chance. The process of learning and doing is what creates engagement—fun."***

That kind of movement is typical. For instance, of the original 24 people hired at the Thames plant when it opened in 1988, today two are vice presidents and group managers, eight are plant managers, and seven are team leaders. And they're all generalists. They know most aspects of our operation inside and out.

***Doesn't eliminating specialists hurt efficiency?***

**Sant:** It might. But we try to reinvent the wheel every time we get a chance. The process of learning and doing is what creates engagement—fun.

**Bakke:** The trade-off is worth it because of the sense of control and total responsibility that people feel when they really own their decisions.

Let me give you an example. We don't have groups of finance specialists, right? But someone has to invest the company's money. The people at the plant do it—it's their responsibility. So in Uncasville, Connecticut, the question went out to all the teams: Is there any group that would like to take a stab at investing the $12 million cash reserve held at the plant? And what was then the maintenance crew—it was a team of about 15 guys—said that they would. They didn't have a clue about how to invest short-term money in the market, but they thought it would be fun to learn.

So they hired a teacher who told them what a spread was, who to call on Wall Street to get the process going, and so forth. After a few weeks of studying, they starting calling up brokers and looking for the best vehicle for investing.

You should have heard them—it was exhilarating. I'd get a little note saying, "Man, you won't believe what happened—such and such broker reneged on the deal! They've been lying to us!"

**Sant:** They went through the process of learning how Wall Street works.

**Bakke:** By the third month, they actually beat the returns of the people who were investing the money for the company's treasury at the home office. They were so proud. My point is this: Did letting the maintenance crew invest that money make a huge difference in our bottom line, for better or for worse? Probably not. But those people will be changed forever. They have become better businesspeople. And there is no other way to do that than by doing. I mean, when do you learn to become a parent? When the baby arrives.

It amazes me—in our society, we tend to treat children like adults, and in the workplace, we treat adults like children. Think about the responsibilities we give kids—the TV programs and movies they watch or the subjects we expect them to know about and understand, like drugs and violence. But then, when they grow up, we put them in work environments where every decision is made for them. We say, "Here are the rules; here are the systems; here is how you do your job." At AES, we're trying to turn that on its head. We're letting adults, like the maintenance crew, take on very big challenges without requiring them to get approvals from senior people before making decisions.

That's not to say there weren't investment parameters for the maintenance crew. There were; they could only invest in A1, A2, or A3 money because the banks don't let us take a lot of risk with cash reserves when they are supporting a project financing. But it's our belief that, almost invariably, people will rise to the level of trust and dignity you invest in them. And the performance of the maintenance crew just proves that.

***Does the maintenance crew still invest money for the plant?***

**Sant:** No, once they figured out how to do it well, it was time to pass the job to other teams. Now groups within the plant bid on it from time to time. And, by the way, we don't have a maintenance crew anymore at that plant. Their work is all distributed to the other teams. As we've said, we're trying not to separate operations and maintenance.

***AES has high expectations for its employees—they have to embrace the company's values, take full responsibil-***

***ity for important decisions, and have the desire and ability to become well-rounded businesspeople. How is hiring handled, then, in particular without an HR department overseeing the process?***

**Bakke:** By and large, plants do their own hiring. We rarely use headhunters, and we really don't recruit much. And we seldom hire people directly into senior levels. People typically come to work in the plants, and they grow with us.

Hiring the right people is essential. The whole system would fall apart if we didn't have a lot of people who were passionately excited by our values or who didn't care about becoming businesspeople. But we've been very lucky over the past few years. We are really fortunate in that we have a huge pool of applicants. We've done well, and people are attracted to that. And I think there is a good feeling out there about us. People who work for us tell their friends about how we operate, and that gets them interested.

***"If you're interested in moving up in a traditional hierarchy, you're not going to choose to work at AES."***

And so we usually have lots and lots of people to choose from; we're able to really pick and choose the people who are likely to understand what it means to be an AES person. And I think that there is also quite a bit of self-selection going on. If you're interested in gaining power or moving up in a traditional hierarchy, you're not going to choose to work at AES.

The same thing can be said about people who are fearful of ambiguity or don't like to make decisions. They usually don't apply here for jobs. We attract people who want to be treated as responsible adults, who say, "I want to be a teacher, a nurturer, a servant-leader." They are typically people who are ready to make decisions and be held accountable for them.

**Sant:** It's important to point out that we very rarely hire primarily for technical ability. We put that factor second in the evaluation process and really focus on cultural fit. And there is a lot of peer review. Teams interview candidates, and there are multiple meetings in which they try to get the sense of the person and whether he or she will be comfortable in the AES environment. (For a sample of AES interview questions, see "What Does 'Fun on the Job' Mean to You?" at the end of this article.)

**Bakke:** We've made our biggest mistakes in hiring when people have said "We need someone with such and such expertise" and put cultural fit second. We've been much better off when we've hired people who don't just accept our values but are evangelical about them. I am always amazed at how well some people who have just been hired understand what we are doing and how well they manage to spread the news, so to speak.

For instance, we purchased six plants in Kazakhstan over the past 18 months. We control about 30% of the electricity-generating capacity in that country. Our team has done an incredible job of explaining to the government that capitalism doesn't have to be "gangsterism," which is how some of the people there perceive it. Our people have been able to demonstrate to the government and to the people working in the plants we have acquired what AES is all about—how we do business and how we represent a different version of capitalism. And these are people who haven't worked at AES for all that long. Some of them have only been with us six months, but they get the values, and they improve on them. It's fantastic.

### *How do you approach compensation and performance evaluation?*

**Sant:** Both have evolved over the years as we've tried to get our ecosystem working properly—that is, consistent with our philosophy. Right now, I'd say we're at a stage where roughly 50% of a person's compensation is based on technical factors such as our financial performance and safety and environmental impacts. The other 50% is based on how well people, individually and as a group, understand and adhere to our four shared values—fairness, integrity, social responsibility, and fun.

**Bakke:** We base our evaluations on a couple of factors. First, everyone who works in a plant that's at least 50% owned by AES, all 10,000 of them, fills out a survey on values every year. I read the results of every single one. It helps me and other leaders see where people are, for instance, acting selfishly—putting themselves first, before the other stakeholders. A few years ago, I noticed that a lot of people from the same plant wrote in their surveys, "Why do we have to buy plants abroad? We should just stay in the United States and provide jobs to Americans." From that, I could tell that the plant manager and team leaders there were not doing a good job of making our mission to meet needs *in the world* understood. And those attitudes also called into question whether people were adhering to the principles of fairness and social responsibility. Were year-end reviews and compensation affected? I think so, at least for company leaders and in the companywide corporate bonus plan.

And second, I visit a lot. I listen to people in the company, and I look to see if people are holding on to power or if they are passing it around. If I hear a team leader proclaiming how happy he is that he finally has the authority to make decisions, I get a little concerned. I ask team members, "Who is actually making the decisions around here? Are you making them or is it the team leader or even some other plant leader?"

Once I found that leaders in a Northern Ireland facility had put a limit on purchases by individual team members. That is, team members had to get approval before they purchased anything that cost more than £2,000—about $3,200. Approval processes are inconsistent with our principles. They take the fun—the responsibility and therefore the mental and emotional engagement—out of work. In fact, I would like to see approval limits abolished at every level of the company—not just for $2,000, but for $2 million or $200 million.

I hope that plant managers and team leaders are asking themselves the same kinds of questions that I ask, and making the same kinds of assessments. Sometimes those assessments, including year-end performance reviews, are done in groups. Each team member will evaluate his or her own performance—in terms of technical skills and on commitment to the principles—and then team members will affirm or critique the review, or sometimes do both.

**Sant:** The next step may be having individuals set their own compensation. One of our group managers is beginning to experiment with that now. The team is based in London, but it covers central Asia, principally. Each senior team member was asked to set his or her own salary this time. It worked well, but the team will decide next year whether to continue the practice.

***When people evaluate one another in a group setting, you might expect a lot of tiptoeing around bad performance: "If you don't criticize me, I won't criticize you."***

***Or you might find that some individuals savage others in order to look better.***

**Bakke:** I am sure that happens to some extent around AES, but not frequently. Over time, people learn that that kind of behavior is not acceptable. Some of it goes back to hiring. The kind of people who engage in those types of behaviors don't often come here, or at least they usually don't last here very long. The people who stay are the ones who say, "I want to be better. I want the group to be better." And they evaluate themselves and others in that vein.

**Sant:** And you have to remember that, at the very senior levels of AES, we've been together a long time. Of our top 20 people, 17 have been working here for a decade or more. We know one another really well, and trust is a big thing among us. And that is transferred to the rest of the organization. We are supportive of one another.

**Bakke:** But *supportive* doesn't mean glossing over someone's problems. Evaluation meetings can be very intense. We push one another. We want to help one another be the best we can be in stewarding resources to meet the world's need for electricity.

**Sant:** We'd eventually like to see everyone in the company involved in this kind of evaluation session. Right now, the sessions are used mainly for some salaried people. Incidentally, we would like to eliminate hourly work at AES. About 50% of our people are salaried now, but we hope to change that soon, so that there won't be any more hourly workers at AES, anywhere in the world.

***What's wrong with an hourly wage system?***

**Sant:** What are you saying when you pay someone an hourly wage? You're saying, "We only care about the physical time you spend in the plant. We don't trust you, so you have to punch a time clock." That attitude is left over from the Industrial Revolution, and that's not the way we feel.

When you pay someone a salary and make them eligible for bonuses and stock ownership, you are saying, "Our assumptions about you are no different from those we have about the plant leader. You can and should bring your brainpower and soul—your whole person—to work." In effect the company is saying, "You're a part of this organization; you have the same worth as everyone else."

At this point, about 50% of our workers who used to get paid by the hour have converted themselves to salary, and we hope that close to 100% will choose that approach eventually. Generally, once people try it, they love it. They're free to do, to be, to understand work in a whole new way. They see themselves differently—as real businesspeople.

***So far, you've described the mechanics of AES in terms of its organizational structure and its approach to hiring and compensation. What other managerial practices make empowerment work?***

**Bakke:** There's the incredibly important matter of free and frequent information flow. I don't know how we'd function without it because it undergirds everything we do. When people are making big decisions on the front lines, it's not as if they are doing so in a vacuum. They shouldn't be. We have lots and lots of corporate memory, and it's crucial for people to be able to access it.

We have very few secrets at AES. Even the details of potential acquisition decisions are shared. Personal compensation issues are confidential, but we're not even sure why that has to be the case.

But besides compensation levels, all financial and market information is widely circulated. That's why for SEC purposes, every one of our people is considered an "insider" for stock trading.

Some people are worried about how public we are with our information; they're concerned it's going to get leaked to competitors. But we think that's a risk worth taking because, otherwise, how would our people become businesspeople? You need information to make good decisions.

**Sant:** But it's not just that we put all our information out there. The system works because people volunteer information—they share knowledge.

**Bakke:** For example, a business development manager named Flora Zhou was chosen to lead our efforts in Vietnam last year. She was putting together a bid to the government—the deal involved supplying a region of Vietnam with about 700 megawatts of electricity for 20 years. Flora had a couple of other people working with her, but she was going to make the final call on the dollar amount of the bid. We knew price was very important to the government. In fact, price would probably account for about 70% of the final decision.

So Flora put together an e-mail that detailed what she was planning to bid and why, and sent it to about 200 or 300 people within AES. She received lots of advice and comments in return, but in general, most people thought her proposal sounded fine.

But a group manager in Central America, Sarah Slusser, had experienced a similar situation with a plant in the Yucatán—there were overlapping technology issues. She sent Flora a three-page e-mail that contained a wealth of information about what to pay attention to with that technology.

A few days later, Flora made the bid, and it was the lowest by two-tenths of a percent. (Nonprice factors are still being evaluated, so the overall winner has not yet been chosen.) Did Sarah tell her the exact dollar amount to bid? No. But she and many others around the company, including plant leaders and board members, gave her the best information and judgments they had to inform her decision. They shared everything they knew with her.

***Do people share knowledge about the principles as well?***

**Sant:** I often get e-mails or phone calls from people asking, How do you see this dilemma? What would you do in this situation? The questions are usually about fairness and integrity. They may sound like they're only about business, but they're not.

For instance, last summer we were working on the acquisition of a power station abroad. Along the way, a question arose about what had been agreed upon during the negotiations. The sellers had one point of view; we had another. But after some discussion, it became apparent to us that the sellers were more right than wrong about their recollection of the negotiations.

So the dilemma became, Do we admit that the sellers are right and go ahead based on their view of events? Or do we keep trying to get some important terms into the purchase and sale agreement that we had overlooked—or not explicitly included—during the negotiations? All the internal e-mails and phone calls about this matter centered on the question of integrity. Would we be acting with integrity if we continued to ask for our desired terms? Eventually, the team answered no. But the discussion leading up to that answer took many turns that helped us to better understand our value of integrity—what it meant in action.

***The notion of accountability seems to greatly influence the way AES runs. How does that work? What would happen, for instance, if Flora Zhou loses a bid?***

**Bakke:** There is no penalty, per se, for losing a bid, but an AES person would be unlikely to receive a bonus if we didn't win the business we were bidding on. And although losing a bid can be a mistake, so can winning a bid in which the economics turn out to be less than satisfactory. For instance, we had a person who bought a hydroelectric plant in Argentina and, based on how successful that transaction appeared to be on the pro forma financial analysis, he received a substantial bonus. He then went on to buy a second plant in Latin America, which looked like it was going to do well, too. But when the time came for a bonus for the second deal, the first plant in Argentina was in trouble. Part of it was not his fault. It didn't rain, and a hydroelectric facility needs water. But he hadn't built that possibility into the pro formas, nor had he built in the possibility that the market price for electricity would fall to the extent that it did. Overall, his projections for returns on the investment had been too optimistic. So he basically gave back his bonus on the first deal by not taking a bonus on the second deal, even though he deserved one.

***"We had a very tough year in 1992—not economically, but in the more important area of values."***

Take another case. We had a very tough year in 1992—not economically, but in the more important area of principles and values. There was a major breach of the AES values. Nine members of the water treatment team in Oklahoma lied to the EPA about water quality at the plant. There was no environmental damage, but they lied about test results. A new, young chemist at the plant discovered it, and she told a team leader, and, of course, we then were notified. Now, you could argue that the people who lied were responsible for the breach and were accountable, but the senior management team also took responsibility by taking pay cuts. My reduction was about 30%.

**Sant:** We said, "It's our fault. Obviously, we didn't train those people properly or hire the right ones or choose the right leader." I mean, if it had been one person falsifying reports, we could have made the case that he or she was a bad seed. But with nine people, we had to accept that the problem was systemic. We demoted the individuals involved, and they took temporary pay cuts. Most of them eventually left, but those who accepted the discipline admitted their parts in the breach. They've stayed with the company and are doing well.

***"It is okay to make most mistakes. We are all human. It's part of AES's values to accept mistakes."***

**Bakke:** We especially hold ourselves accountable for safety. At some of our plants, if there is one accident, everyone's bonus is cut by 25%, two accidents means a 50% cut, and by the third, there's no bonus for anyone. Last year we all took a cut in our companywide wealth-sharing plan because there were four fatal accidents at our plants—one in China, two in Kazakhstan, and one in Pakistan. We could have received up to 12% of our salaries in our bonuses. It was a perfect year from a lot of perspectives for us, but we decided that those deaths had to be accounted for, and we gave ourselves a 10% reduction in the bonus. It didn't matter where the deaths occurred or that no one who died was an AES person; in three cases, they were contractors, and in one case, a civilian. Our company is a community, and we are accountable to the world as one.

### *Are all mistakes penalized financially?*

**Bakke:** Serious ones, yes. The same mistake made a second or third time, yes. But a mistake made as you learn, without significant consequences, of course not. It is okay to make most mistakes. We are all human. It's part of AES's values to accept mistakes, as long as people own up to them.

**Sant:** And you would be amazed at how quickly people support and forgive one another here. I haven't seen that in many organizations. In other places, when someone makes a mistake, the company is really punishing, and peer support vanishes.

### *Why is AES so forgiving?*

**Bakke:** Maybe because of the humility that says, "We've been there. We've been on the front lines and made big decisions and big mistakes." I mean, on our first two or three projects, Roger and I really screwed up.

**Sant:** We should have been hung out to dry.

**Bakke:** Our first plant, in Pasadena, Texas, lost $20 million a year for about six years. And then we bought prototype turbines for the Placerita plant in California in 1984, and they kept cracking and eroding. And we also bought an oil field near there at the same time that lost us about $20 million. That whole investment lost money for years, until people at the plant figured out how to fix it. Now it's doing very well, very little thanks to us.

**Sant:** The good news about owning up to your mistakes right away is that it is so much easier to move quickly to find a creative solution. You don't sit around wasting time trying to figure out whom to blame.

***If AES's mechanics push responsibility and accountability away from corporate headquarters—what is left for you to do? How does empowerment redefine the role of the leader?***

**Bakke:** We—and all AES leaders—end up having four roles. The first is to be advisers. We probably get more deference than we deserve, but people listen to our opinions.

The second is to be chief guardians of the principles. We don't have to play this role very often because the principles are well known. In fact, most of the time, our people guard the values without any input from senior people. For instance, our people in Indonesia had to decide whether to give 15% of a project there to a member of the Suharto family. The payment wasn't illegal, but people in our company decided that paying such a "tax," which basically was bribery, did not fit with our principles of fairness and integrity. We never did get a project in Indonesia. Roger didn't make that decision, and neither did I. So the guardian role really plays out most often when we write and teach.

Our third role is to be chief accountability officers. If no one else holds you accountable, or if for some reason the teams don't hold themselves accountable, we're the backup players. We ask, "Well, how did it go? How did we do?"

**Sant:** But as we've said, it's really hard to come up with a time we have had to do that. So this role ends up being something else: we are AES's chief accountability officers to the outside world. We answer for the company to people who question our values or challenge our integrity. That happened after the Oklahoma incident. And it happened earlier that same year. We wanted to build a cogeneration plant in Jacksonville, Florida. It would supply electricity to a local utility and steam to an adjoining paper mill. After we got the permits to go ahead, a member of the community claimed that we had lied about our plans, and she led a charge against us in the media. At issue was the number of boilers we would use at the paper plant. We had said we would shut the existing mill boilers, but later we said we were considering cleaning them up and then reopening them. Whichever approach we took, the amount of emissions—which was critical to the whole debate—would be exactly the same.

For six months, AES was really under fire. I spent most of my time in Jacksonville, and Dennis went to the state capital, Tallahassee. We really poured everything we had into defending the honor of the company. We were fighting to protect our values and what we stood for. The veracity of our principles was called into question. Eventually we prevailed, and the governor and cabinet gave us the go-ahead to continue building, but by that time, we were so worn down by the experience that we sold our share in the plant and moved on.

*What's your fourth role?*

**Bakke:** We're the chief encouragers. We celebrate with AES people. We attend orientations and plant openings. We give the speeches at five-year anniversary parties.

**Sant:** People always say they don't have time to celebrate because they're too busy, but stopping and remembering is really important. What is work if you don't see the meaning in it? You have to celebrate the meaning in it.

***Are you saying you have dispensed with the main leadership role at traditional companies: making the major decisions that no one else wants to, or can, make?***

**Bakke:** This year I made two decisions, which was one more than last year. I made the decision about how many regional groups we would have and who would lead them. Those were big decisions, so I took six months to make them. I really played them out, because if you only make two decisions a year, you want to play them for all they are worth.

As for the rest of the decisions (strategic, planning, capital allocation, and so on) that needed to be made for AES—well, they were made by the people out there who are right on top of the problems or issues or opportunities.

***You've described how empowerment works, but the question arises: Why empower in the first place?***

**Sant:** Certainly not for strategic reasons. You see that a lot these days—companies that endorse empowerment or operate with socially responsible principles claim that it is not only the right thing to do but also makes brilliant strategic sense. For us, the part about brilliant business sense is beside the point. The point is improving the world—even saving it. It's the right thing to do.

I think capitalism could be different. I think that we have to reinvent capitalism around a sense of mission—it can improve society by improving the lives of people.

**Bakke:** My own sense is that we are not so much trying to reinvent capitalism as we are trying to go back to something. Corporations were originally created for very specific purposes. Back in the eighteenth century, when the government gave a corporation a charter, it was to do something for the public good, like build a canal or a bridge. But that emphasis has shifted over the years. When I give speeches nowadays and ask the audience, "Why do businesses exist?" 75% of the people say the same thing, regardless of whether I am at Harvard Business School or a Christian college. They say, "To make money."

***"I think that we have to reinvent capitalism around a sense of mission—it can improve society."***

Capitalism is in great jeopardy if people hold on to that notion. Companies have to exist primarily in order to *contribute* to society, to meet its needs. Businesses have to help people live better lives. They have to operate in ways that help communities cohere and thrive.

***You both believe businesses should benefit society. Why?***

**Sant:** Dennis and I actually come from somewhat different places on this one. My ideas about empowerment are based on experience, stimulated significantly by an integration of theory X and theory Y and by Bob Waterman, our long-time board member and author of *In Search of Excellence*. Quite a while back, I started thinking about when I had the most fun at work, and I realized it was when I was given responsibility and accountability, when I had the chance to make a difference. I figured there might be other people like me. My original notions about social responsibility arose because I had seen a lot of environmental irresponsibility. I headed up the energy conservation program at the Federal Energy Administration from 1974 to 1976. It was there that I came to believe that people couldn't keep doing unsustainable things—in terms of pollution, mainly. There had to be some answers to the question, How can we create a society that would stop stealing from the capital of the planet? And I realized that business played an important role. Companies could handle social responsibility in an integrative way, not tack it on at the end of their thinking about operations, like some kind of afterthought. That is, business could build social responsibility into its values and practices.

That's why, for instance, to offset our carbon dioxide emissions in Connecticut, we funded the planting of 52 million trees in Guatemala and why, to offset emissions from a plant in Hawaii, we gave a grant to preserve 144,000 acres of forest in Paraguay. In Pakistan, however, we learned that the environment was not necessarily the number one social problem in that country. So we've built four schools. We've built a school for 1,000 children in China. We want our company to do everything it can to be a responsible part of our communities—proactively, not reactively.

**Bakke:** My belief in empowerment comes from my Christian faith, but many of my beliefs are not inconsistent with the fundamentals of Buddhism, Judaism, and Islam. I recently got a letter from an AES person who was leaving us to join a Buddhist monastery. She wrote, "Thank you for giving me an opportunity to work in a company where I could fully live out my values." So there are commonalities across the faiths.

Personally, I start with the book of Genesis, which teaches us that we are put on earth to glorify God by stewarding our resources for ourselves and for others. Our nonhierarchical structure and our desire to engage the wholeness of people comes from my belief that God created each one of us in his image. The Bible teaches that each person is holy, special, and unique. We are creative, accountable, trustworthy—and fallible. That's where forgiveness comes in. God set up the world with forgiveness. We are to work for wholeness and justice, integrity and fairness. And social responsibility comes from a requirement to love our neighbor as ourselves. Treat each person with respect and dignity. In essence, I would love to get the workplace as close to the Garden as possible, knowing we can't. But I shouldn't stop trying.

***"I would love to get the workplace as close to the Garden as possible, knowing we can't."***

***You want to make money at AES, though, don't you?***

**Bakke:** Profits are a consequence of doing a good job of stewarding and of meeting a need. And they are essential so that we can pay shareholders the returns they deserve. Profits in and of themselves, however, are not the central purpose of AES.

**Sant:** You have to make money because the enterprise can't be sustained unless you do. And profits often measure how effectively you are carrying out your mission.

**Bakke:** We don't operate with the traditional notion that the company exists, first and foremost, for the benefit of the shareholders. Shareholders are one important constituency of our company, but they are not the most important. We have many other stakeholders: AES people, our customers, the communities we build and run our plants in, suppliers of debt and other services, the governments of the countries where AES operates. I used to say that our competitors were stakeholders, too, but my colleagues laughed at me and made me stop. But I still think it's true. Our competitors are critical to us because they make us better, and they make us credible. If we don't do things better—if we don't surpass them in meeting the world's needs for safe, clean, reliable electricity—then we'll disappear, as we should.

***The ecosystem of empowerment that you've described differs from the way most companies today are organized and managed. Do you think that AES is unique?***

**Sant:** Yes, but I hope not for long. The world will work better if people are empowered. But I would not recommend that other businesses adopt only our mechanics. They'd have to adopt some shared values first, because the mechanics flow from them. You can't have one without the other. But if companies adopt a set of shared principles, then the mechanics can be put in place. It takes time and commitment, though, because it's not easy to give up power. And it's very easy to fall back into the conventional way of doing things.

**Bakke:** That's what happened after the incident in Oklahoma. You know, our stock dropped $400 million in one day—one-third of the company's value at the time—and the board and others started saying, "Okay, your experiment is over. It failed. It's time to revert to the traditional way of doing things." And the people at the plant agreed. They went to shift supervisors like conventional industrial facilities have; a deputy plant manager was installed; and a bunch of functional departments were put in—such as environmental regulation, planning, and safety. And the plant manager basically fired me. He called me and said, "Please don't come out here anymore."

I spent about four months talking to people all over AES. I asked, "How can we stick with our fundamental principles and not move backward?" Finally, step by step—and there were a lot of conversations that took place—we agreed that we believed in our principles, and we would not waver. As for the Oklahoma plant, it didn't happen all at once, but eventually the people there undid what they had done to themselves. They got back to the AES way.

***"At the end of the day, the team members aren't going to say, 'It's not my job.' Everything is their job."***

***Can you think of an industry or situation where empowerment isn't applicable or appropriate for safety or regulatory reasons?***

**Bakke:** Just the opposite. People think empowerment is a big free-for-all or something. That everyone is just "empowered" to do what he or she wants. But people are more accountable for their actions in our system than that, and maybe more accountable at AES than at many typical, traditional, hierarchical companies. The greatest difficulty any organization will have following the AES approach—including AES—is getting its leaders to freely and consistently give up the power to make decisions.

**Sant:** There are life-and-death decisions in our work all the time. There is always danger when you are working with awfully high temperatures and pressures, as we are. But empowerment makes it safer—not riskier. If a team feels it is fully accountable, it will take more responsibility than if it feels that its boss is accountable. At the end of the day, the team members aren't going to say, "It's not my job." Everything is their job. Very little slips through the cracks.

It's true that in some industries you need accumulated knowledge to do your job right. But we take care of that at AES by making sure people reach out and talk to one another, get advice, and share information. The Flora Zhou story is evidence of that, and there are hundreds of stories like hers.

***As AES has expanded—both by building plants abroad and by forming alliances—have there been new or unexpected challenges?***

**Sant:** We haven't had the problems opening plants internationally that people predicted. For some reason, people thought that our principles and our way of doing things couldn't work overseas. But we haven't really experienced anything like that.

**Bakke:** In fact, sometimes our non-U.S. employees "get" AES faster than Americans do.

**Sant:** That's not to minimize that people are different in Hungary or Kazakhstan. But all people are innately the same. People from different countries and cultures may take longer to trust—to trust AES leaders, to trust the AES approach, and to trust themselves to take responsibility.

**Bakke:** People become who they are based on their microenvironments—not just the country they grew up in. They are formed by how they grew up—their families and their communities.

I was at Stanford a few months ago talking with the business school students, and by and large it was the American students who were saying, "Oh, you can't export AES's values abroad." But the foreign students were saying, "That will work just fine in my country." And it's been gratifying for me to see that the foreign students appear to be right. Certain values transcend cultural and religious borders, and AES is based on some of them.

*And alliances?*

**Sant:** The weakest part of our company is that we don't work with other companies very well. We're starting to figure it out, but we're not there yet.

**Bakke:** If you believe strongly in a particular set of principles, and if you practice your business in accordance with them, it's very difficult to have a partnership with a company that does not believe in them. As we said in our 1997 annual report, we're still not very good at working with partners who don't share our ideas, and I'm not sure we ever will be. You can't mix oil and water.

**Sant:** We have a new situation in Los Angeles that is working well—it's with Williams Companies. Williams gives us natural gas, and we convert it to kilowatt-hours. Then they take them back and sell them. It's not a formal partnership. It's a contractual relationship, and I think it may be a better approach to working together than anything we've done yet. Maybe when it's all said and done, we'll find their culture is great and we will mix well together, but we don't have to test that in this case.

**Bakke:** I mean, we would love to change the world. But we're not going to do it with a gun; we're not going to force it. We're going to try to do it with ideas. We hope people will hear our story and see how we do things and that, eventually, business will start to change.

**Sant:** And hopefully, the world will change, too.

*What will happen to AES after you're gone?*

**Sant:** I'm spending more than half my time outside of AES now, devoting most of my time to chairing the World Wildlife Fund and Sant family foundation. We call it the Summit Foundation, and it's devoted to assisting organizations to protect the environment and stabilize world population.

**Bakke:** I don't have any plans to leave soon. But that's a hard question. Sometimes I worry that the company will be run by someone who doesn't feel as strongly about our central tenets as I do. But in reality, that's not a worry of much merit. There are likely to be a number of people from inside the company who will build on what we have started and take AES's people to a whole new level of excellence. But doing that will necessarily involve staying true to the principles.

**Sant:** As we see it, empowerment without values isn't empowerment.

**Bakke:** It's just technique.

---

## What Does "Fun on the Job" Mean to You?

IN ORDER TO MAINTAIN AES's empowerment ecosystem, it is critical to hire the right people. Because the company's mechanics are so tightly coupled with its principles, it is essential that every employee, new and old, embrace those principles. It follows, then, that the interview process, largely conducted by teams at the plant level, is extensive—even exhaustive—and focused on cultural fit. Only when a candidate appears to have the makings of an "AES person" is his or her technical expertise examined.

The goal of the interview is to determine whether the candidate will eagerly accept decision-making responsibility—that is, be held completely accountable for results, both good and bad. In addition, the company seeks candidates who believe that it is the responsibility of business to improve the lives of people and society in general. Candidates should be able to demonstrate their commitment to fairness and integrity, two key AES values. And finally, they should define fun the AES way, as a full mind-body-soul engagement with work well done—not just the celebration afterward. The following are questions typical of an AES interview.

- Should everyone be treated equally? Explain.
- What do you do when something needs to be done and no procedure exists?
- What self-improvement efforts are you making?
- Recall a time when people around you weren't being totally honest. What did you do?
- What does "fair" mean to you? How important is fairness?
- For what have you been counseled about the most?
- What is the most difficult situation you have faced? What did you feel? How did you react?
- Describe two important achievements.
- Tell me about a time when a decision was needed and no supervisor was available.
- What kinds of rewards are most satisfying to you?
- What does "fun on the job" mean to you?

**Originally published in January–February 1999**
**Reprint 99109**

# Unleashing the Power of Learning

## *An Interview with British Petroleum's John Browne*

STEVEN E. PROKESCH

## Executive Summary

JOHN BROWNE BELIEVES THAT all companies battling it out in the global information age face a common challenge: using knowledge more effectively than their competitors do. And he is not talking only about the knowledge that resides in one's own company. "Any organization that thinks it does everything the best and that it need not learn from others is incredibly arrogant and foolish," he says.

British Petroleum's chief executive, who engineered the revival of BP Exploration and Production and poised BP for spectacular growth, never accepts that something can't be done and is always asking if there is a better way and if someone might have a better idea. Under his leadership, BP is doing the same. And no matter where knowledge comes from, Browne says, the key to reaping a big return is to leverage that knowledge by replicating it throughout the organization so that each unit is not learning in isolation.

To create an environment conducive to such learning, BP's leaders have taken a number of steps. They have built an extrememly flat, decentralized organization: there is nobody between the general managers of the business units and the company's top management. They have installed processes to institutionalize breakthrough thinking and tie people's jobs to creating value. Finally, they have exploited advances in information technology and designed learning networks in order to encourage people to share knowledge.

---

*With his talk of "the shrinking half-life of ideas," "virtual team networks," and "breakthrough thinking," John Browne sounds more like a Silicon Valley CEO than the head of the giant British Petroleum Company. Then again, BP–with its flat organization, entrepreneurial business units, web of alliances, and surging profits–is starting to look and act like a vibrant Silicon Valley enterprise. Such comparisons may seem wild, but Browne thinks that all companies battling it out in the global information age face a common challenge: using knowledge more effectively than their competitors do. And he is not talking only about the knowledge that resides in one's own organization. "Any organization that thinks it does everything the best and need not learn from others is incredibly arrogant and foolish," he says.*

*BP is a radically different company today than a decade ago, when it was an unfocused mediocre performer whose businesses extended to minerals, coal, animal feed, and chicks. The vast majority of its oil and gas output came from large fields in the North Sea and in Alaska's North Slope whose production was beginning to decline. BP's reserves were shrinking, and its finding and development costs were so high—three times higher than those of its major competitors—that it had difficulty making any money on new fields.*

*Today BP is the most profitable of the major oil companies. Its debt, which had grown as a result of acquisitions, unrestrained capital spending, and the buyback of a big block of shares from the Kuwaiti government, has been slashed to $7 billion from a 1992 peak of $16 billion. BP now has strong positions in such important oil and gas regions as the Gulf of Mexico, South America, western Africa, the Caspian Sea, the Middle East, and the Atlantic Ocean west of the Shetland Islands. BP's finding and development costs are now among the lowest in its industry. Its output is growing at about 5% per year. And even without additional discoveries, the company has the wherewithal to maintain its reserves for at least ten years.*

*Organizationally, BP is much smaller and simpler than it was a decade ago. It now has 53,000 employees—down from 129,000. Before, the company was mired in procedures; now it has processes that foster learning and tie people's jobs to creating value. Before, it had a multitude of baronies; now it has an abundance of teams and informal networks or communities in which people eagerly share knowledge.*

*Much of the credit for BP's recovery goes to David Simon, Browne's predecessor, who became CEO in June 1992, when BP's board ousted Robert Horton. Besides putting BP's financial house in order, Simon drove home two messages: performance matters, and teamwork is crucial for improving performance.*

*But the man who engineered the revival of BP Exploration and Production (BPX) and poised BP for growth is Browne, who headed BPX from 1989 to July 1995, when he succeeded Simon as CEO. Browne, who is 49, grew up in BP–almost literally. His father had worked for the company, and, after graduating from the University of Cambridge with a degree in physics, the younger Browne followed suit, joining as an apprentice petroleum engineer. While in his thirties, he ran BP's important Forties field in the North Sea. In 1984, he became treasurer, and in 1986, he moved to Standard Oil of Ohio, in which BP had a majority stake. Browne helped Horton rationalize the company before it fully merged with BP.*

*Browne is the kind of person who never accepts that something can't be done and who is always asking if there is a better way or if someone might have a better idea. Under his leadership, BP is becoming the same kind of company. One case in point: BP's unconventional idea to merge its European fuel-and-lubricant business with Mobil's. The landmark deal struck last year offers an opportunity to create one healthy first-tier player out of two second-tier players whose prospects in the mature, oversupplied market seemed bleak.*

*Browne discussed his ideas with Steven E. Prokesch, who conducted the interviews in London and New York while a senior editor at HBR. Prokesch is now codirector of idea development at the Boston Consulting Group in Boston, Massachusetts.*

---

***Some management thinkers believe we are entering an age of globalization in which building and leveraging***

***knowledge will be the key to success. Do you agree?***

Absolutely. Knowledge, ideas, and innovative solutions are being diffused throughout the world today at a speed that would have been unimaginable 10 or 20 years ago. Companies are only now learning how to go beyond seeing that movement as a threat to seeing it as an opportunity. We see it as a tremendous opportunity.

***How will the diffusion of knowledge affect the rules of competition?***

Learning is at the heart of a company's ability to adapt to a rapidly changing environment. It is the key to being able both to identify opportunities that others might not see and to exploit those opportunities rapidly and fully. This means that in order to generate extraordinary value for shareholders, a company has to learn better than its competitors and apply that knowledge throughout its businesses faster and more widely than they do. The way we see it, anyone in the organization who is not directly accountable for making a profit should be involved in creating and distributing knowledge that the company can use to make a profit.

***"Learning is at the heart of a company's ability to adapt to a rapidly changing environment."***

The wonderful thing about knowledge is that it is relatively inexpensive to replicate *if* you can capture it. Most activities or tasks are not onetime events. Whether it's drilling a well or conducting a transaction at a service station, we do the same things repeatedly. Our philosophy is fairly simple: Every time we do something again, we should do it better than the last time. This year, drilling will account for more than $3.8 billion in capital expenditures on exploration and production. We drill lots of wells. If we drill each well more efficiently than the last one, we can make a lot more money—which is exactly what we're trying to do.

We haven't been at it too long, but already we're reaping fantastic gains. Deepwater drilling is a good example. We have a big acreage position in the deep water of the Gulf of Mexico, where drilling is an enormous technical challenge. The water there is between 2,000 and 8,000 feet deep, and then you have to drill 7,000 to 12,000 feet below the seabed to reach hydrocarbons. Because the water is so deep, you can't affix anything to the seabed, and no human being can go down that far. So you have to use special vessels to drill. They are very expensive, and because it's fashionable to be drilling in this area, they're becoming even more expensive. In 1995, we spent 100 days on average drilling deepwater wells. We now spend 42. How did we do it? By asking every time we drilled a deepwater well, What did we learn the last time and how do we apply it the next time? And we learned not only from our own people but also from contractors and from partners such as Shell.

***What kinds of learning are crucial? What are the challenges in maximizing them?***

There are a variety of ways you can learn how to do something better. You can learn from your own experience. You can learn from your contractors, suppliers, partners, and customers. And you can learn from companies totally outside your business. All are crucial. No matter where the knowledge comes from, the key to reaping a big return is to leverage that knowledge by replicating it throughout the company so that each unit is not learning in isolation and reinventing the wheel again and again.

The conventional wisdom is that excelling in incremental learning is a science—a matter of installing the right processes—while excelling in breakthrough thinking is more of an art. I disagree about the latter: I think you *can* install processes that generate breakthrough thinking. We have.

Another conventional view is that it is harder to tap implicit knowledge, which is the experiential knowledge locked inside someone's head, than explicit knowledge, which can be captured in a database. But that hasn't been our experience. We have had great success in fostering the personal interactions you need to mine implicit knowledge.

Our challenge has been getting people to systematically capture the information the company needs in order to be able to use both explicit and implicit knowledge repeatedly. In the case of explicit knowledge, that means recording the actual data. In the case of implicit knowledge, it means keeping a record of the people who have the know-how to solve a problem so that others can find them when the need arises. The trouble is that both tasks are boring. So we've got to figure out how to make them exciting and enjoyable. We've made progress, but we have a long way to go. (See "Sharing Knowledge Through BP's Virtual Team Network" at the end of this article.)

***"A clear purpose allows a company to focus its learning efforts in order to increase its competitive advantage."***

***What's the most important rule for building an effective learning organization?***

A business has to have a clear purpose. If the purpose is not crystal clear, people in the business will not understand what kind of knowledge is critical and what they have to learn in order to improve performance. A clear purpose allows a company to focus its learning efforts in order to increase its competitive advantage.

What do we mean by *purpose?* Our purpose is who we are and what makes us distinctive. It's what we as a company exist to achieve, and what we're willing and not willing to do to achieve it. We are in only four components of the energy business: oil and gas exploration and production; refining and marketing; petrochemicals; and photovoltaics, or solar. We're a public company that has to compete for capital, which means we have to deliver a competitive return to shareholders. We're in a highly competitive global industry in which cost matters. We serve a global market that offers growth opportunities, and we want to grow. But in our pursuit of exceptional performance and sustained growth, there are certain financial boundaries we will not cross and values we will not violate. The values concern ethics; health, safety, and the environment; the way we treat employees; and external relations.

***Was a fuzzy purpose one of the root causes of your previous problems?***

We needed to redefine exactly what we were trying to do. The world never stands still, and a company has to keep moving on. That is the only way you can maintain control of your own destiny.

Although the perceived challenge at the end of the 1980s was replacing our falling reserves, there was no framework for doing so. Our capital spending was going up, up, up. We were exploring in a lot of places—50 to 60 countries around the world. But many of those efforts were unlikely ever to deliver a competitive return on capital. For example, we were exploring in the Netherlands, the home country of Royal Dutch/Shell. The way I see it, any company that explores there had better have a solid idea of why it might stand a better chance of finding something worthwhile than Shell, which is a very good company.

In other words, many of the things we were doing were not distinctive. We were not insisting on getting value for the money we invested. You cannot live like that for long. The capital markets won't let you.

A few of us on BP's senior management team were convinced that the world had changed in some fundamental ways that offered us a chance to create a radically new future. We realized that advances in technology and opening markets were creating opportunities to find and develop big new oil and gas fields—those with 250 million barrels or more—in such places as South America, Vietnam, the Caspian Sea, and the Atlantic Ocean west of the Shetland Islands. In addition, there was demand for that oil and gas: global consumption was growing, mainly because of growth in the emerging economies.

Ultimately, we decided to focus on finding giant oil and gas fields: the cost of finding, developing, and operating them is low, they offer growth potential, and they would allow us to earn a high return on capital. We decided to focus on just 20 countries, which made us think long and hard about which were the best opportunities. And we agreed to get rid of everything else that couldn't make a material difference or offer growth potential—everything not distinctive.

**Distinctive** ***is a word you use a lot around BP. What precisely do you mean by it?***

Things that are hard to copy, that give us a competitive edge or serve as a competitive barrier. At BP, four key elements create distinctiveness: assets and market shares, technologies, organization, and relationships.

Distinctive assets are assets that, given your culture, management, and knowledge, allow you to produce outstanding returns and achieve sustainable growth. For BPX, giant oil and gas fields are distinctive because of their low cost and because there are so few of them. For BP Oil—our refining and marketing group—large market shares, stations with high volumes, and refineries that perform in the top quartile of their markets are distinctive. Our share of the European fuel-and-lubricant market wasn't big enough to be sustainable, which is why we merged that operation with Mobil's. The partnership should deliver savings on the order of $400 million to $500 million per year, provide a platform from which to enter the new growth markets of central and eastern Europe, and give us the opportunity to learn a lot from Mobil.

***"You can't create an enduring business by viewing relationships as a bazaar activity."***

We mean several things by *distinctive technologies.* The first is obvious: patented processes that give us an advantage in competing for customers and partners, and in gaining entry to new markets such as China. In our chemicals business, our patented processes for making acrylonitrile, acetic acid, and polyethylene are distinctive. Second, distinctive technologies are those that can help us increase productivity and cut costs year after year. Third, distinctive technologies are those that can help us capture and share knowledge. For example, information technology is the key to allowing people to work with others—to share knowledge and solve problems—across the boundaries of countries and companies and corporate structures.

By allowing us to stay on the leading edge, distinctive technologies of all kinds help us attract and retain the most talented people. If we aren't regarded as leading-edge, why would a graduate join us instead of Microsoft or Intel? We need the most talented people in order to build a distinctive organization.

### *What are the qualities of a distinctive organization?*

Its people are highly motivated, understand exactly what they have to do to help create great value, can see the results of their actions, and have a sense of ownership. They excel at building and using knowledge capital, which means accessing and applying knowledge that exists both inside and outside the company. They excel at forging distinctive relationships.

### *Why does a company need distinctive relationships?*

We need to form them with partners, suppliers, customers, and the countries in which we operate so that we all can work together to maximize value. You can't expect others to share their knowledge and resources with you fully unless you have a strong relationship with them.

You can't create an enduring business by viewing relationships as a bazaar activity—in which I try to get the best of you and you of me—or in which you pass off as much risk as you can to the other guy. Rather, we must view relationships as a coming together that allows us to do something no other two parties could do—something that makes the pie bigger and is to your advantage and to my advantage.

One case in point is how Schlumberger, the oil-field-services company, developed a special device for us called a logging tool. We were drilling lots of horizontal wells, and it occurred to us that we didn't know what was going on. Was the entire horizontal well producing? Did we drill too much or too little? There was no available device that could tell us, which was surprising, because the whole industry was drilling horizontal wells. So we went to Schlumberger and said, "We have one or two rudimentary ideas on how to do this. But we'd like our scientists and your scientists to get together because we need the tool, and this could be a wonderful business opportunity for you. Recognizing that there's a little risk, we'll pay you for some of the development and we'll use some of our wells to test the tool."

And that's what we did. Some of our people went to Schlumberger's research laboratory to work with its people. Once they understood the technology, they built a prototype, which looked like a piece of pipe you put down wells. It was vast—150 feet long. Honoring our side of the agreement, we put it down one of our wells. For one horrible moment, it got stuck, which meant we'd lose not only the tool but also the well. Eventually it was okay, and we proved the concept. We asked Schlumberger to make it a bit smaller and to make it available to us first before offering it to everyone in the world. The result was that we got a tool that has taught us a lot about what we needed to do to make horizontal wells even more effective, and Schlumberger got a new business.

### *What does it take to build distinctive relationships?*

The most important aspect of any relationship is understanding what your partners hope to get out of it and to work hard to help them achieve that goal. It is the key to transforming a contractual relationship into a genuine collaboration.

Second, you have to deliver on your promises reliably and consistently. Your promises have to be realistic, and you need to move heaven and earth to keep them.

Third, you never build a relationship between your organization and a company or a government. You build it between individuals. Our people have to have real authority. We can't cut them off at the knees. They must be people who can deliver.

Fourth, all relationships worth anything are open and flexible. In other words, you must invite people in, try to discuss the problem or opportunity, and say, "How do we solve it jointly?" If you say, "Here is my solution. I'm having a great relationship with you if you agree, and I won't have a relationship with you if you disagree," then the relationship is not to mutual advantage.

Fifth, you have to approach an opportunity—which should be the basis of every relationship—with humility. You have to recognize that others may actually know more than you do about something—that you can learn from them. For example, we know we can learn a lot from Mobil about operating refineries and marketing lubricants. Shell has taught us much about deepwater drilling, and we hope it has learned something from us.

Finally, you build relationships for the very long term. Even in tough wholesale businesses such as airplane fuel, this approach can give you an edge. How? You reject the notion that it is a commodity business. Then you try to build relationships with the airlines based on creating a long-term mutual advantage. And you strive to share long-term plans so you can service the airlines' planes effectively all over the world.

Of course, you cannot have a strong relationship with everyone. But in general, long-term relationships are the most profitable ones. Think about going into a new country. If you do just one piece of business in that country, how on earth are you going to recover the setup costs? So you have to think, What's the business after that? How do I get a sustainable position? The obvious answer is by building strong, long-term relationships.

***One of the most challenging jobs in trying to create a learning organization is teaching the organization to learn. Could you talk about the steps involved?***

In our case, the first was to instill the belief that competitive performance matters—that producing value is everyone's job and that to produce value you need to focus so that you don't get distracted by things that aren't central. BP is not a collection of financial assets. It is a combination of assets and the activities, people, and learning needed to extract maximum value from those assets. The way I see it, there are two justifications for keeping each piece of business that we own. The first is that our company has the culture and processes to manage each piece better than anybody else. The second is that the pieces inside the company learn from one another and consequently can do things better together over time.

For people to learn how to deliver performance and grow BP, we had to make them feel that, individually and collectively, they could control the destiny of our businesses. Of course, there are aspects of our business that are outside our control—oil prices, for instance. But there are many others that we can control. To drive home that message, we talk a lot about *self-help,* and we rigorously track and publicize the results that it produces.

What is self-help? It is about how we control the cost structure, get more bang for the investment buck, upgrade the quality of products and services, and improve relationships with suppliers and customers. It's about getting people to develop an intimate understanding of the structures of their businesses' margins and how they compare with those of their competitors. It is a big reason why we split the company into some 90 business units and why we now share numbers and plans much more widely. In the past five years, self-help has generated $4 billion worth of permanent improvements.

***Isn't it often difficult to get people to focus on the importance of creating value and not to operate on autopilot?***

Yes. In the late 1980s and early 1990s, we had a problem, which I suspect many companies—especially big ones—share. People often took an incremental or piecemeal approach to a project or an opportunity. A good example is the replacement of the pipeline in our Forties field in the North Sea. It was an old 32-inch line that was past its useful life. We decided we would build a 36-inch pipeline because we

***"Ideally, teaching and learning should occur both within the parts of our business groups and across the different groups."***

thought we could attract a lot of other business, the cost difference was very small, and we could make it last longer by using new corrosion and emission technologies.

We were going along merrily for two months when the guy running the North Sea group came to me and said, "Sign this." It was a request for $150 million to build a new platform because, as it turned out, we couldn't put the new pipeline on the old one. So I said, "I'll tell you what: we'll build it, but we'll spend only $100 million, and this is the last time something like this happens." The final cost was $110 million.

Such experiences made us realize that we had to install a disciplined planning-and-approval process to make people look at the whole: the entire project, how it fits into the strategy, and the return that must be generated in order to make the project worthwhile. If people focus from the outset on that whole, they will then devote themselves to learning what needs to be done to achieve the total goal.

***What you're saying is that you had to teach people that the way to get maximum value was to excel at learning. How did you put in motion such a learning process?***

By setting competitive and comparative targets and challenging people to achieve them. To get people to learn, you need to give them a challenge. Setting a target is crucial even if you don't actually know whether it's fully achievable—because in times of rapid change, you have to make decisions and get people to step outside the box.

One process that we employ to promote learning and drive performance is not that unusual. It involves understanding the critical measures of operating performance in each business, relentlessly benchmarking those measures and their related activities, setting higher and higher targets, and challenging people to achieve them.

Another, more unusual process involves breakthrough thinking. When we assess opportunities, we ask, If the usual approaches or business system cannot produce the return on capital that we need, are there others that can? Let's challenge the boundary. The development of the Andrew field, which changed the economics of developing oil and gas fields in the North Sea, demonstrates the dramatic results that that kind of thinking can produce. (See "Breakthrough Thinking: How to Develop the Undevelopable" at the end of this article.)

> ***"The role of leaders at all levels is to demonstrate to people that they are capable of achieving more than they think they can."***

***What is the role of a leader in institutionalizing breakthrough thinking?***

The top management team must stimulate the organization, not control it. Its role is to provide strategic directives, to encourage learning, and to make sure there are mechanisms for transferring the lessons. The role of leaders at all levels is to demonstrate to people that they are capable of achieving more than they think they can achieve and that they should never be satisfied with where they are now. To change behavior and unleash new ways of thinking, a leader sometimes has to say, "Stop, you're not allowed to do it the old way," and issue a challenge.

The development of our Wytch Farm oil field near Poole, England, is a case in point. In the late 1980s, BPX was producing from onshore wells when we discovered that the field extended significantly offshore into Poole Harbor, an area of particular scientific interest and one of the most beautiful places in Europe. The question over the next few years was how to produce that oil. Because accessing the oil from land seemed technically infeasible—a horizontal well of that distance had never been drilled—the initial, knee-jerk plan was to build an artificial island in Poole Harbor and drill from that, even though it would require an act of Parliament.

Everything was going forward: a bill had been introduced, and brochures, a lobbying strategy, and a plan aimed at defusing the anticipated attacks by environmental groups had been prepared. The estimated cost was just about tolerable, but it was high, and you had to factor in what would really happen once the plan was under way: the costs would just go up and up.

Then my management team said, "Stop! We're not going to do this. We've got to figure out another way." We assembled a multidisciplinary team to tackle the challenge, borrowing the best people from wherever they resided in BPX.

The team decided that developing the offshore reserves without an artificial island was perfectly doable if we could make a breakthrough in horizontal-drilling technology and drill under the seabed from the existing onshore locations. And the team did it. It didn't try to leap mountains in one stride. Instead, it took the best available technologies and then, slowly, step by step, went beyond them. In the end, the wells were five miles long—the longest drilled in the history of the oil industry—and saved us $75 million.

This was the sort of innovation that people would come up with when we challenged them. And before too long, it became contagious. Without prodding, people began to ask themselves, Where can I innovate? Or they would realize on their own, This isn't a good idea—let's try something different. So, contrary to what some may believe, you *can* institutionalize breakthrough thinking.

### *How do you make sure that people do not inadvertently damage the business when they make mistakes during the learning process?*

By experimenting, which is integral to learning. I think it's impossible to predict what will happen when you deploy a strategic thought inside an organization. I don't think you can predict people's behavior. Therefore, you've got to experiment. You've got to see what people actually do. You've got to see how the idea works. You've got to learn how to build something with a bit of track record, which you then can apply more widely.

We are taking that approach toward developing a chain of integrated food-and-fuel convenience retail sites in Britain with Safeway, the supermarket chain. We said to Safeway's leaders, "We think it's a terrific idea. It looks as though we could have a mutually advantageous relationship with you. We can see the strategy. We've got real estate you want. We've got a nice brand. You've got a wonderful system for delivering fresh food." The trouble is that neither of our companies really knows the other. Ideally, we'd like to do 100 sites. But first we'll conduct an experiment with 8 sites, set some targets, and measure the results. If the experiment works, we'll go full steam ahead. In that way, we'll get to know each other. We'll see whether we can have a relationship.

In all the organizational changes in which I have been involved, I've said, "Rather than take a cataclysmic approach, let's try it, see how it works, understand what we've learned, and only then apply it more widely." Then the challenge is to excel at building on that knowledge and to apply the cumulative knowledge quickly and broadly throughout the organization.

***How did you design an organizational structure to promote learning?***

We have built a very flat team-based organization that is designed to motivate and help people to learn. We've divided the company up into lots of business units, and there is *nothing* between them and the nine-member executive group to whom they report, which consists of the three managing directors of our business groups and their six deputies. The organization is even flatter than my description makes it sound, because each of the managing directors and his deputies work as a team in dealing with the business units.

We've worked with the managers of each business unit to create an annual performance contract that spells out exactly what they're expected to deliver, and we review their progress quarterly. In addition, we've developed all sorts of networks to encourage the sharing of knowledge throughout the organization. Finally, we've integrated our technology organization with the business units so that it is working with them both to solve the most important business problems and to exploit the most important business opportunities. Previously, the technology organization was a separate fiefdom, focused on invention. To be fair, we did get some good innovation—in gas-to-

***"However good a company is, it can't expect to possess more than a tiny fraction of the world's best technology."***

liquid technology, for example. But sometimes the technology group's inventions were pretty peripheral, such as pills for making pink flamingos pinker. Overall, we were not getting good value for our investments.

In the last five years, we've refocused our technology people on application. Now their mission is to access the best technology wherever it resides inside or outside BP and apply it quickly, cutting costs and time to market. However good a company is, it can't expect to possess more than a tiny fraction of the world's best technology. Moreover, I suspect that if a lot of companies rigorously analyzed whether their proprietary technologies really do provide a competitive edge, many would be surprised by the number that don't. For example, we had assumed that proprietary seismic technology for finding new oil fields gave us an advantage in exploration. But on closer scrutiny, we realized that it did not. For one thing, the reality is that we often have to share it either with partners or with state-owned oil companies in order to gain access to frontier areas. For another, we have found that our people's ability to combine and apply technologies—not the technologies themselves—is often what gives us an advantage.

***How does your new organizational structure compare with the old one?***

It's a far cry from the complicated structure we used to have, which included enormous regional organizations, matrix management, and huge staffs in the headquarters of the company and of the business groups. Excluding the people in the financial and oil-trading organizations, the headquarters of the company and of the business groups now employ only 350 people—an incredibly small number for a company with revenues of $70 billion. In

1989, that total was about 4,000. Having lived through the days of huge staffs and complicated structures, my predecessor, David Simon, and I passionately believed that we had to push decision making out to where it could be managed most effectively—to the business units—and that we had to get rid of the clutter so that learning could flow.

We divided the company up in this fashion so that people would not feel like part of a great, big organization, so that they would not get lost, so that they would have pride of ownership. We wanted people to be able to see the impact of their actions on the business's performance. So we designed the organization in a way that let everyone see clearly how things are done and understand what each person's role is in getting it done. It's based on processes, not tasks or hierarchies. Processes linked to a purpose are powerful at changing behavior because people can see what they're aiming for.

I'm not talking just about operational processes. I mean management processes, too. When a managing director and his deputies review the past performance and future plans of every business unit quarterly with its general manager, the message is sent that performance matters. That's an assurance process. We also have a strategic process for ensuring that the units are constantly creating lots of business options for the future and are constantly sorting through them and improving them.

***It sounds as though you're saying that life is complicated and we need to make it simpler.***

That's right. A team of people focused on a coherent bit of a big, complex business can develop the kind of intimate knowledge of the business that's needed to maximize performance and to create the options necessary for building the future. They can work the assets harder than a large organization can, and they're much less likely to sit on those assets if they can't be made to perform or don't make sense. It's a structure that allows people to have many face-to-face interactions and to form deep personal relationships, which are critical in a learning organization.

Whether a business unit is mainly an asset, such as an oil field, or is developing downstream markets in central Europe, we make sure that it is big enough to justify putting a really great manager in charge of it. But the units are small enough that their leaders can have one-to-one interactions with people rather than town-hall-style meetings—which, in my view, are an ineffective way of communicating.

A virtue of this organizational structure is that there is a lot of transparency. Not only can the people within the business unit understand more clearly what they have to do, but I and the other senior executives can understand what they're doing. Then we can have an ongoing dialogue with them and with ourselves about how to improve performance and build the future.

A leader must not only grasp the big picture but also be able to break it down into bits that are real for individuals. Take the issue of growth. I have to remind myself constantly that the manager of our business unit in central Europe, for example, doesn't care about macro numbers—that global oil consumption is going up by 2% per year, gas consumption by 3%, and demand for the kind of

***"If you named a boss, you'd have a hierarchy, and hierarchies hamper the free exchange of knowledge."***

chemicals we produce by 6%. She wants to know which specific growth opportunities she should pursue in, say, Poland.

***To leverage learning, knowledge must flow among business units. I would think the challenge is to create links among the units to promote that flow without recreating the organizational clutter of the past. How have you tackled that challenge?***

Information technology is one solution. In addition, we have made much progress in forming what you might call learning communities. For example, each of the 40 business units that constitute BPX belongs to one of four peer groups. The members of each peer group wrestle with common problems. They have a lot to learn from one another. They share technical staff. And they all are equals.

***There is no boss?***

No, because if you named a boss, you'd have an organization and a hierarchy, and hierarchies—or, more specifically, the politics that accompany hierarchies—hamper the free exchange of knowledge. People are much more open with their peers: they are much more willing to share and to listen, and are much less likely to take umbrage when someone disagrees with them. Regardless of the team, if it isn't operating on a peer basis, it's not going to get the right interactions. It might sound like fantasy, but I truly consider myself only the first among equals in the top management team.

***What is the basis for each peer group?***

For both BP Oil—our refining and marketing group—and BP Chemicals, the basis is functional. For BPX, the basis is the life cycle of the exploration-and-production business. The members of one peer group are the business units that are finding new fields. Their concerns include getting governments to grant them permission to explore, improving seismic analysis, and minimizing the number of dry holes. The members of the second peer group are the units that develop the fields. They're the big spenders. This year, they have a capital budget of $2.2 billion, which they are free to manage on their own. Their issues range from how best to deal with corrosion problems to how to immerse a workforce in a new area in BP's health-and-safety culture. The members of the third are the units whose fields are at plateau production. They are the steady income producers—the money powerhouses. And those in the fourth are all operating old or late-life fields. Their challenges include squeezing as much as they can out of the fields, cutting costs as the fields tail off, decommissioning wells, and reducing the size of the workforce.

I think knowledge is really flowing among the units *within* each of our three main business groups: BPX, BP Oil, and BP Chemicals. Now the challenge is to get that knowledge flowing more easily *across* the groups.

***Why is it important to create networks linking dissimilar businesses? Do they have much to learn from one another?***

Different eyes see different things, and many of those businesses have much more in common than you might think. If you step back far enough, there isn't too much difference between operating an offshore oil platform, an ethylene plant, and a refinery. And, regardless of whether their equipment is similar, many units face common problems, including health, safety, and environmental issues, as well as how to conduct business in difficult places like Colombia and Algeria.

Given the free flow of information around the world these days, applying the same values and standards everywhere is necessary for building sustainable relationships. If we don't do that, there's a growing danger that when we try to get a new piece of business in, say, China or Venezuela, people there will say, "You do it differently in Alaska. Why aren't you doing it the same way here?"

So it is important for knowledge to flow both within and across our business groups. To that end, we're currently striving to turn BP's 350 most senior people into a team. They control assets, functional knowledge, and other resources. They are the people who really can get things done.

***I have been struck by how you have been trying to create a culture that is comfortable with change and embraces continual innovation. How do you keep an organization from ossifying?***

In order to be in control of your destiny, you must realize that you will stay ahead competitively only if you acknowledge that no advantage and no success is ever permanent. The winners are those who keep moving. We have tried to instill this attitude in our people.

We've tried to make it not only acceptable but also expected that people look for a better way or grab the best ideas from wherever they find them. We've benchmarked ourselves against our own industry for a long time. Now we also expect people, when they're setting targets or challenging a boundary, to look beyond the oil industry to whichever industry does something best. For example, we've learned a lot from the automobile industry about procurement, which has helped us lower the cost of building service stations. And we went to the U.S. Army to learn about capturing and sharing knowledge.

***"Information technology is wonderful because it makes riches possible without formal structures."***

Another way to prevent ossification is to minimize the amount of organizational structure. Information technology is wonderful because it makes rich exchanges possible without formal structures.

Finally, to create an effective learning organization, you don't bolt things down. You let the organization and the ways in which it learns evolve. If you don't, organizational structures can become obstacles to the free flow of knowledge and can become disconnected from the business purpose. When I headed BPX, I set new targets every two years or so and then changed the structure and some of the people in order to deliver the targets. Why? Because I think you have to impose discontinuous change until you can see that the organization will discontinuously change itself. I think there's a limit to how much continuous improvement can achieve.

It may seem obvious, but I think many managers lose sight of the fact that the business purpose should determine the organizational structure. Many managers who have tried to transform their companies have made the mistake of reorganizing or trying to build teams *before* they had clarified and communicated the purpose. At

BPX, we didn't begin to think about the kind of organization we wanted to build until we had a firm idea of where we wanted to be and of the disciplined approach to business that we wanted to take. What is the point of building anything unless you know what the business purpose is?

We're still constantly changing the organizational structure to fit our business purpose. For example, when the British gas market recently underwent deregulation, we spotted an opportunity. If we could develop the ability to respond to temporary surges in demand for gas from industrial buyers, we could make a tidy profit. But it meant that our marketing people had to be in direct contact with our people operating our production platforms. In a matter of days, we set up a gas management board composed of production and marketing people to find ways to supply that demand. We were able to move faster than any of our competitors, and that gave us an advantage.

***Isn't there a danger that the learning networks you are encouraging will end up creating organizational complexity?***

I don't think so. One of the beauties of the networks is that they are not organizational structures per se. Having said that, one of the virtues of BPX's peer groups is that they institute change because a business unit changes its peer group when it enters a new phase of its business's life cycle.

In general, we don't think of our business units as permanent structures. When we were setting them up, we did a lot of experimenting to get them right. We're still constantly scrutinizing them to make sure they serve their business purpose, maximize learning, and help teams perform. If they don't, we change them: we split them up or combine them.

### *What part does strategic planning play in a learning organization?*

Our strategic planning process is designed to keep ideas flowing and to stimulate thinking. We see strategy as applying a series of frameworks that help us constantly reexamine what we are doing relative to what the world can offer and what our competitors are doing. We start with our purpose. Who are we? What sorts of businesses are we in? What are the characteristics of those businesses? What are the limits—in terms of our values and financial boundaries—to the sorts of activities that we are prepared to undertake? What makes our company distinctive?

Using those frameworks to shape our dialogues with our people, we begin to create a strategy that lives because it is always changing as competitive dynamics change or as we understand them more clearly. You don't build a distinctive business by talking about it once a year or once every two years, and then writing a document and putting it in a drawer. You build it by having the company's leaders talk about it with the people in the business units—both formally quarter by quarter and informally even more often. Then people from the top of the company down to the business unit are thinking about it all the time and adjusting what they do every day in light of reality. It's a tremendous way to get people to grasp what is really happening in every component of the company and to help them avoid falling into the trap of thinking of strategy as something fixed or as cash flow analyses, with one answer and one answer only.

Given the uncertainty in the world, strategy cannot be about gambling on one possible outcome five or ten years down the road. Grand master plans have a habit of not being fulfilled. In my view, strategy is about buying the right options that will give us a shot at competing in the future—that will give us the right to play if we decide we want to when it becomes clearer what the game is about. To create the kind of distinctive asset base and market positions that allow one to outperform the competition and generate great returns requires a continuous process of developing strategic options, applying skills and technology to stretch their potential, and regularly winnowing them, choosing only the best.

### *What is the role of top management in the learning organization?*

The most senior leaders in any company do only a very few things. Ultimately, they have to make decisions on the organizational architecture and the way forward. They set policies, standards, and targets, and create processes to ensure that people achieve or adhere to them. It is while those processes are being carried out that learning should take place. What determines whether it does is the questions leaders ask and the way they approach what is going on. Leadership is all about catalyzing learning as well as better performance.

Leaders have to demonstrate that they are active participants in the learning organization. You can't say "Go do it" without participating. Take the part I play in the quarterly reviews of business units' performance contracts. After the managing director of each group and his deputies have reviewed all their business units, I'll review their performance by exception. By that I mean that if something is very good or very bad, we'll focus on it to try to understand what happened and how the business units in question and other business units can learn from that exception. It's one of the ways I'd like to think I help capture and transfer learning in the company. Learning is my job, too, which, by the way, is why I recently joined Intel's board.

*What do you think you can learn from Intel?*

Intel is a high-tech company that has to contend day in and day out with incredibly rapid change. It really has to survive on its ideas—it has to rely on its intellectual property for the next thing it does for the customer. And it has to excel at motivating creative people who have technical skills. BP also is a high-tech company. We're trying to deal with a rapidly changing environment. And we, too, need to attract and motivate highly skilled technical people. There's plenty Intel can teach us.

I find it extraordinary that people buying personal computers actually ask whether Intel is inside. People don't ask whether BP is inside. Maybe someday they will.

---

## Sharing Knowledge Through BP's Virtual Team Network

AT A TIME WHEN *BUREAUCRACY* is a dirty word, it's easy to forget that a bureaucracy historically served two essential purposes: it connected the leaders of a corporation to their businesses, and it allowed the businesses to exchange critical knowledge. Have times really changed? Is it possible to have it all: a flat, decentralized, global corporation that excels at learning and has leaders who are deeply engaged in helping to shape the strategy and drive the performance of the businesses? "Yes," declares John Browne, chief executive of the British Petroleum Company. "Advances in information technology now make it possible." Or so BP hopes to prove.

BP today is amazingly flat and lean for a corporation with $70 billion in revenues, 53,000 employees, and some 90 business units that span the globe. There is nobody between the general managers of the business units and the group of nine operating executives who oversee the businesses with Browne. The way Browne sees it, the people in the business units—those closest to BP's assets and customers—should run their businesses. And in his view, the value that can be derived from sharing knowledge, not geographical location, should drive the interactions among the business units, which is why he deems BP's *virtual team network* to be so important. The aim of this computer network is to allow people to work cooperatively and share knowledge quickly and easily regardless of time, distance, and organizational boundaries.

The network is a rapidly growing system of sophisticated personal computers equipped so that users can work together as if they were in the same room and can easily tap the company's rich database of information. The PCs boast videoconferencing capability, electronic blackboards, scanners, faxes, and groupware. But that's not all.

These PCs, as well as all the other 35,000-odd basic PCs in the company, are connected to an intranet that contains a rapidly growing number of home pages. Everyone at BP now has the capability and authority to create his or her own home page. The corporate philosophy: Let a thousand—or a million—home pages bloom.

As of July, the intranet sites contained approximately 40,000 pages of information.

The home pages serve a number of purposes. There are sites where functional experts describe the experience they have to offer. There are sites for sharing technical data on the muds used as drilling lubricants and for sharing contacts and information about programs and processes available to reduce the amount of pipe that gets stuck in wells. There is a site where people concerned about how to get computers to handle the transition to the year 2000 can exchange ideas. Every technology discipline has its own site. The general managers of all the business units in BP Exploration and Production (BPX) have their own home pages, where they list their current projects and performance agendas.

"If it's easy for people to connect, communicate, and share knowledge, they will do it. If it isn't, they won't," says Kent A. Greenes, BP's virtual teamwork project director. To make it easier, BP is experimenting with a variety of approaches: making videos that can be seen on the network; creating electronic yellow pages that can be searched in a variety of ways; and encouraging people to list interests, expertise, and experiences that they are willing to share with anyone wishing to contact them.

During the recent development of the Andrew oil field in the North Sea, BP used the virtual team network to pass on lessons from the revolutionary project in real time. BP and its contractors and suppliers cooperated to an unprecedented degree to figure out radical ways to cut the cost and time of the project. Using the virtual team network, the project's participants briefed other BP units, partners, and contractors in places as far away as Alaska and Colombia on how they made critical decisions.

The network began in 1995 as a $12 million pilot program in BPX. About a third of the money was spent on behavioral scientists, who helped the people in the pilot programs learn how to work effectively in a virtual environment. "We realized that virtual teamwork required a new set of behaviors," says John B.W. Cross, BP's head of information technology. "It required people to be cooperative and open about what they know, and not possessive about information."

Browne felt that BP should not force the network on people. Rather, he believed that if people saw its benefits, they would ask for it. He was right. "After about six months, we suddenly found out that a lot of people in other groups were asking, `How do we get one?' Some people were bootlegging and buying the stuff on their own," he says.

In 1996, Browne made the virtual team network available to everyone at BP under one condition: they had to pay for it out of their own budgets. "They said, `We don't mind. It's just fantastic.' It's an example of how an organization changes itself when it sees something worthwhile," Browne says. As of July, the virtual team network had grown to 1,000 PCs, and Cross expects it to soar to 10,000 by 1999. The network links teams working in the Gulf of Mexico with teams working in the eastern Atlantic near the Shetland Islands, and the PCs are installed in refineries and chemical plants from Indonesia to Scotland.

BP also is extending membership in the virtual team network to outside organizations. For example, the company is using the network to improve the way it works with partners such as Shell in the Gulf of Mexico, and with contractors such as Brown & Root in the North Sea.

Some of the benefits of the virtual team network are easy to measure:

- A big drop in the person-hours needed to solve problems as a result of improved interactions between land-based drilling engineers and offshore rig crews.
- A decrease in the number of helicopter trips to offshore oil platforms.
- The avoidance of a refinery shutdown because technical experts at another location could examine a corrosion problem remotely.
- A reduction in rework during construction projects because designers, fabricators, construction workers, and operations people could collaborate more effectively.

BP estimates that the virtual team network produced at least $30 million in value in its first year alone. But this estimate does not take into account the harder-to-measure benefits–such as the ability to see the whites of someone's eyes in a videoconference when he or she makes a commitment.

Each member of BP's top management team and each general manager of the business units has at least one virtual team workstation. Browne has two: one in his office and one in his London home. They allow him to be in two places or more at the same time, he says, describing how he recently participated in separate management conferences in Johannesburg and Singapore from his office. "We had great discussions," he says. "We talked about BP, where it was going, the constraints, the issues that they had. Had I not had the network, what would I have done? Tried to bend my schedule to the point of absurdity? Sent a videotape?"

Browne believes that effective leadership requires personal relationships. It requires continual conversations about competitive dynamics, performance, and corporate values. "These technologies allow the center to stay engaged with the business," Cross says. "Without them, John's organizational model is not sustainable.".

---

## Breakthrough Thinking: How to Develop the Undevelopable

SINCE DISCOVERING OIL AND GAS in the Andrew field in the North Sea in 1974, the British Petroleum Company had repeatedly tried in vain to figure out how to develop it economically. In the late 1980s, the company even had considered writing down and selling its majority interest in the field. But in 1990, BP had a compelling reason to try again. The 1986 collapse of world oil prices and the discovery of giant oil fields in other parts of the world threatened the viability of the North Sea as a major oil-producing region. If BP could develop Andrew, with its estimated 112 million recoverable barrels of oil and 3.8 billion cubic meters of gas, then it also would be able to tackle profitably the mostly small fields that remained to be developed in the region. The challenge was a big one: at a time when oil prices were $14 per barrel, BP was demanding a 25% return on investment.

John Browne, then head of BP Exploration and Production (BPX), personally picked Andrew. He was one of the many senior BP executives who had had first-hand experience with its problems. As a young engineer, he had participated in an unsuccessful effort to find a profitable way to bring the field into production. In 1990, he was trying to reinvigorate BPX and turn it into a place where innovation was a way of life. He saw the challenge of developing Andrew as an opportunity to demonstrate the power of breakthrough thinking. The approach: set a seemingly unattainable target and see how close you can get to attaining it by assigning the best minds to the problem, scouring the world for the best ideas—doing whatever it takes.

Browne assembled a team of people from a wide range of disciplines and with different perspectives from both inside and outside BPX's North Sea group in the hope that the resulting dialogue would produce fresh ideas. At first, the team saw the challenge mainly as solving a petroleum-engineering problem. But by the end of 1991, the team was stuck. Even with the latest technology, it saw no way to develop the geologically complex field for less than $675 million, which was still too high a price to make the project attractive. The team's plan called for only incremental changes to the traditional cost-plus approach of paying contractors a fixed amount above the actual cost. It was not breakthrough thinking. Browne wouldn't let the team off the hook. "You've got to do what you initially promised to do," he said.

The team, which was being coached by JMW Consultants—a firm in Stamford, Connecticut, that specializes in helping teams make breakthroughs—began to broaden its thinking and reconsider every aspect of the problem. Instead of looking only at technology for the solution, how about looking at BPX's relationship with its contractors? Instead of continuing the practice of treating contractors as adversaries and playing them off against one another, how about treating them as allies? How about giving them a financial interest in the project's success and encouraging them to work together to challenge costs, seek the best value, and innovate?

The approach turned out to be the breakthrough that BPX needed. It set an extreme target of $405 million to send the message that the project would require revolutionary new attitudes, practices, and ideas. It chose seven contractors that it deemed to be committed to pioneering a new open and collaborative approach. And it promised to let them be full-fledged partners in designing and managing the project and to let them carry it out without the heavy oversight that had been typical of BPX. Then it asked this "alliance" team to come up with a project proposal, which itself was a big departure from usual practice. Generally, BP staff would have completed all the conceptual engineering-design work and a significant amount of the detailed engineering design. Only after the project had received the go-ahead would the contractors have been brought in.

"In this case, BPX said, `We don't have a feasible project yet. But if you help us figure out how to do it, we'll promise to give you the work,'" recalls Norman C. Chambers, at the time a senior executive at Halliburton's Brown & Root division, the contractor responsible for management support and much of the design work and procurement.

In November 1993, the alliance submitted a detailed proposal to develop Andrew for $560 million, with oil production to begin in January 1997. Some of its innovative suggestions included employing 12 horizontal wells rather than 19 vertical wells and, instead of building the deck in modules and then assembling them offshore, building a single integrated deck that could be installed onto the offshore structure with a single lift. The plan also called for testing and certifying process equipment onshore, and reducing the total cost of equipment and materials by 30% through minimizing inspections, making direct purchases instead of going through agents, and giving suppliers the freedom to figure out the best way to meet functional specifications.

The estimate passed the 25% hurdle rate. But BP analysts, using historical cost data, gave the plan only a 38% probability of being completed within the estimate—below the 50% probability typically required for approval. But the alliance proposed an innovative risk-and-reward scheme, which persuaded BP and four other oil companies with minority stakes in the field to give it the go-ahead in February 1994. Under the arrangement, the contractors would absorb 54% of any cost overruns, with a maximum exposure of $40 million. If the project came in below $560 million, the contractors would receive more than 50% of the savings in addition to their normal pay. "We knew that unless we did something extraordinary, we would lose money, but we were willing to take the risk because of BP's commitment to doing something different," says Chambers, who is now president of Halliburton Energy Development, another Halliburton division.

The project came in at just below $444 million and was completed more than six months early. The seven contractors shared a bonus of nearly $69 million.

How did the alliance do it? By setting stretch targets and challenging every aspect of the schedule and the design, thereby slashing the cost of materials. By reducing the duplication of effort significantly. By incorporating all the skills and knowledge from the alliance's eight members into the design process, thereby ensuring that the designs could be constructed efficiently and that costly rework would be eliminated. By building a three-dimensional computer simulation of the whole project, drastically reducing the number of person-hours spent on design work. By making the contractors largely responsible for meeting quality and safety specifications. By greatly standardizing equipment, materials, and components. By working with suppliers as partners. And by breaking with convention and inviting the certifying authorities and the crew that would operate the platform to be on-site members of the team.

One dramatic result: once the three-deck platform was installed, it was producing within days rather than the usual months. "Every day, we challenged every assumption," Chambers says. "We analyzed anything that might reduce costs and speed up the development time. And we made breakthroughs practically every day."

The alliance approach is now spreading throughout BP. The company has formed similar alliances to develop its oil fields near the Shetland Islands and the Badami field in Alaska, to expand a polyethylene plant in Indonesia, and to refurbish its Grangemouth refinery in Scotland.

"One important thing about Andrew is that it is making money and producing above the design specifications," Browne says. "But it also taught us a new way of doing things by building relationships to mutual advantage with a variety of people. It was a major watershed."

*Some of the information in this insert comes from Terry Knott,* No Business As Usual *(London: British Petroleum Company, 1996), an account of the development of the Andrew field.*

**Originally published in September–October 1997**
**Reprint 97507**

# The Power of Virtual Integration

## *An Interview with Dell Computer's Michael Dell*

JOAN MAGRETTA


## Executive Summary

MICHAEL DELL STARTED his computer company in 1984 with a simple business insight. He could bypass the dealer channel through which personal computers were then being sold and sell directly to customers, building products to order. Dell's *direct model* eliminated the dealer's markup and the risks associated with carrying large inventories of finished goods.

In this interview, Michael Dell provides a detailed description of how his company is pushing that business model one step further, toward what he calls *virtual integration*. Dell is using technology and information to blur the traditional boundaries in the value chain between suppliers, manufacturers, and customers.

The individual pieces of Dell's strategy—customer focus, supplier partnerships, mass customization, just-in-time manufacturing—may all be familiar. But Michael

Dell's business insight into how to combine them is highly innovative. Direct relationships with customers create valuable information, which in turn allows the company to coordinate its entire value chain back through manufacturing to product design. Dell describes how his company has come to achieve this tight coordination without the "drag effect" of ownership.

Dell reaps the advantages of being vertically integrated without incurring the costs, all the while achieving the focus, agility, and speed of a virtual organization. As envisioned by Michael Dell, virtual integration may well become a new organizational model for the information age.

---

How do you create a $12 billion company in just 13 years? *Michael Dell began in 1984 with a simple business insight: he could by-pass the dealer channel through which personal computers were then being sold. Instead, he would sell directly to customers and build products to order. In one swoop, Dell eliminated the reseller's markup and the costs and risks associated with carrying large inventories of finished goods. The formula became known as the* direct business model, *and it gave Dell Computer Corporation a substantial cost advantage.*

*The direct model turned out to have other benefits that even Michael Dell couldn't have anticipated when he founded his company. "You actually get to have a relationship with the customer," he explains. "And that creates valuable information, which, in turn, allows us to leverage our relationships with both suppliers and customers. Couple that information with technology, and you have the infrastructure to revolutionize the fundamental business models of major global companies."*

*In this interview with HBR editor-at-large Joan Magretta, Michael Dell describes how his company is using technology and information to blur the traditional boundaries in the value chain among suppliers, manufacturers, and end users. In so doing, Dell Computer is evolving in a direction that Michael Dell calls* virtual integration. *The individual pieces of the strategy–customer focus, supplier partnerships, mass customization, just-in-time manufacturing–may all be familiar. But Michael Dell's insight into how to combine them is highly innovative: technology is enabling coordination across company boundaries to achieve new levels of efficiency and productivity, as well as extraordinary returns to investors. Virtual integration harnesses the economic benefits of two very different business models. It offers the advantages of a tightly coordinated supply chain that have traditionally come through vertical integration. At the same time, it benefits from the focus and specialization that drive virtual corporations. Virtual integration, as Michael Dell envisions it, has the potential to achieve both coordination and focus. If it delivers on that promise, it may well become a new organizational model for the information age.*

---

***How has Dell pioneered a new business model within the computer industry?***

If you look back to the industry's inception, the founding companies essentially had to create all the components themselves. They had to manufacture disk drives and memory chips and application software; all the various pieces of the industry had to be vertically integrated within one firm.

So the companies that were the stars ten years ago, the Digital Equipments of this world, had to build massive structures to produce everything a computer needed. They had no choice but to become expert in a wide array of components, some of which had nothing to do with creating value for the customer.

As the industry grew, more specialized companies developed to produce specific components. That opened up the opportunity to create a business that was far more focused and efficient. As a small start-up, Dell couldn't afford to create every piece of the value chain. But more to the point, why should we want to? We concluded we'd be better off leveraging the investments others have made and focusing on delivering solutions and systems to customers.

Consider a component like a graphics chip. Five or ten years ago, a whole bunch of companies in the personal computer industry were trying to create their own graphics chips. Now, if you've got a race with 20 players that are all vying to produce the fastest graphics chip in the world, do you want to be the twenty-first horse, or do you want to evaluate the field of 20 and pick the best one?

It's a pretty simple strategy, but at the time it went against the dominant, "engineering-centric" view of the industry. The IBMs and Compaqs and HPs subscribed to a "we-have-to-develop-everything" view of the world. If you weren't doing component assembly, you weren't a real computer company. It was like a rite of passage. You somehow proved your manhood by placing small semiconductor chips on printed circuit boards.

And Dell Computer came along and said, "Now wait a second. If I understand this correctly, the companies that do nothing but put chips on motherboards don't actually earn tremendous profit doing it. If we want to earn higher returns, shouldn't we be more selective and put our capital into activities where we can add value for our customers, not just into activities that need to get done?" I'm not saying those activities are unimportant. They need to get done very, very well. But they're not sources of value that Dell is going to create.

When the company started, I don't think we knew how far the direct model could take us. It has provided a consistent underlying strategy for Dell despite a lot of change in our industry. Along the way, we have learned a lot, and the model has evolved. Most important, the direct model has allowed us to leverage our relationships with both suppliers and customers to such an extent that I believe it's fair to think of our companies as being virtually integrated. That allows us to focus on where we add value and to build a much larger firm much more quickly. I don't think we could have created a $12 billion business in 13 years if we had tried to be vertically integrated.

*Why can you grow so much faster without all those physical assets?*

There are fewer things to manage, fewer things to go wrong. You don't have the drag effect of taking 50,000 people with you. Suppose we have two suppliers building monitors for us, and one of them loses its edge. It's a lot easier for us to get more capacity from the remaining supplier than to set up a new manufacturing plant ourselves. If we had to build our own factories for every single component of the system, growing at 57% per year just would not be possible. I would spend 500% of my time interviewing prospective vice presidents because the company would have not 15,000 employees but 80,000.

Indirectly, we employ something like that many people today. There are, for example, 10,000 service technicians in the field who service our products, but only a small number of them work for us. They're contracted with other firms. But ask the customer, "Who was that person who just fixed your computer?" The vast majority think that person works for us, which is just great. That's part of virtual integration.

***Aren't you just outsourcing your after-sales service? Is what you're describing fundamentally different from outsourcing?***

Outsourcing, at least in the IT world, is almost always a way to get rid of a problem a company hasn't been able to solve itself. The classic case is the company with 2,000 people in the IT department. Nobody knows what they do, and nobody knows why they do it. The solution—outsource IT to a service provider, and hopefully they'll fix it. But if you look at what happens five years later, it's not necessarily a pretty picture.

***"When we launch a new product, our suppliers' engineers are right in our plants. If a customer has a problem, we can fix it in real time."***

That's not what we're doing at all. We focus on how we can coordinate our activities to create the most value for customers.

With our service providers, we're working to set quality measures and, more important, to build data linkages that let us see in real time how we're doing—when parts are dispatched, for instance, or how long it takes to respond to a request for service. We look at our business and see, for example, that over the next ten years we are going to be making lots of notebook computers. Dell might need 20 million flat-panel displays, and some years there will be more demand than supply. Other years, there will be more supply than demand. A few companies are currently making multibillion-dollar investments in the manufacture of these displays.

So we cook up a little deal where the supplier agrees to meet 25% of our volume requirements for displays, and because of the long-term commitment we make to them, we'll get our displays year in and year out, even when there's more demand than supply. The supplier effectively becomes our partner. They assign their engineers to our design team, and we start to treat them as if they were part of the company. For example, when we launch a new product, their engineers are stationed right in our plants. If a customer calls in with a problem, we'll stop shipping product while they fix design flaws in real time.

***"Virtual integration means you basically stitch together a business with partners that are treated as if they're inside the company."***

Figuring out how many partners we need has been a process of trial and error. You learn when you operate on the cutting edge of technology that things don't always work as planned. The rule we follow is to have as few partners as possible. And they will last as long as they maintain their leadership in technology and quality. This isn't like the automobile business, where you find a tire supplier that you will probably stick with forever. Where the technology is fairly stable—in monitors, for example—we expect our partnerships to last a long time. Others will be more volatile. But regardless of how long these relationships last, virtual integration means you're basically stitching together a business with partners that are treated as if they're inside the company. You're sharing information in a real-time fashion.

We tell our suppliers exactly what our daily production requirements are. So it's not, "Well, every two weeks deliver 5,000 to this warehouse, and we'll put them on the shelf, and then we'll take them off the shelf." It's, "Tomorrow morning we need 8,562, and deliver them to door number seven by 7 A.M."

You would deal with an internal supplier that way, and you can do so because you share information and plans very freely. Why doesn't the same sharing of information take place across company boundaries? Buyers are often so busy trying to protect themselves that the seller can't really add a lot of value. Government purchasing is the extreme case, with its overly structured procurement system. Protecting the buyer usually ends up disabling the seller—and both lose.

The technology available today really boosts the value of information sharing. We can share design databases and methodologies with supplier-partners in ways that just weren't possible five to ten years ago. This speeds time to market—often dramatically—and creates a lot of value that can be shared between buyer and supplier. So technology enhances the economic incentives to collaborate.

### *What are the challenges involved in establishing these collaborations?*

The key challenge—and the biggest change from business as usual—is changing the focus from how much inventory there is to how fast it's moving. All computer chips carry a four-digit date code. For example, "97-23" means it was built in the twenty-third week of 1997. You can take the cover off any computer and find out how old its parts are, how long it took to make its way through the system. In our industry, if you can get people to think about how fast inventory is moving, then you create real value. Why? Because if I've got 11 days of inventory and my competitor has 80, and Intel comes out with a new 450-megahertz chip, that means I'm going to get to market 69 days sooner.

> ***"The biggest change from business as usual is changing the focus from how much inventory there is to how fast it's moving."***

I think about it this way: Assets collect risks around them in one form or another. Inventory is one risk, and accounts receivable is another risk. In our case—with 70% of our sales going to large corporate customers—accounts receivable isn't hard to manage because companies like Goldman Sachs and Microsoft and Oracle tend to be able to pay their bills. But in the computer industry, inventory can actually be a pretty massive risk because if the cost of materials goes down 50% a year and you have two or three months of inventory versus 11 days, you've got a big cost disadvantage. And you're vulnerable to product transitions, when you can get stuck with obsolete inventory.

Inventory velocity is one of a handful of key performance measures we watch very closely. It focuses us on working with our suppliers to keep reducing inventory and increasing speed. With a supplier like Sony, which makes very good, reliable monitors, we figure there's no need for us to have any inventory at all. We are confident in putting the Dell name on them, and they work fine. We don't even take these monitors out of the box to test them because we've gotten them to under 1,000 defects per million. So what's the point in having a monitor put on a truck to Austin, Texas, and then taken off the truck and sent on a little tour around the warehouse, only to be put back on another truck? That's just a big waste of time and money, unless we get our jollies from touching monitors, which we don't.

So we went to Sony and said, "Hey, we're going to buy two or three million of these monitors this year. Why don't we just pick them up every day as we need them?" At first, it's a little confusing to the suppliers because you're saying, "Now listen carefully. If you will help us get your product from the end of your line to our customer faster, we won't have any in our warehouse." And the suppliers look at you like you're crazy and not making any sense. They're used to delivering in larger quantities, so at first they think this means you're going to buy less from them. And then the lightbulb goes on, and they realize we'll be buying more because we'll be taking it faster.

***So now you have Sony producing a level supply of monitors for you. What happens next?***

We tell Airborne Express or UPS to come to Austin and pick up 10,000 computers a day and go over to the Sony factory in Mexico and pick up the corresponding number of monitors. Then while we're all sleeping, they match up the computers and the monitors, and deliver them to the customer.

Of course, this requires sophisticated data exchange. Most people are familiar with the way a company like Black & Decker uses information links with the thousands of retailers that sell its products. When a customer in Omaha buys a drill from his local hardware store, the system immediately tells Black & Decker to send another unit of that particular drill to that particular store. So their system has to replenish supply, unit by unit, to thousands of outlets. From the supplier's point of view, Dell is dramatically simpler. Our orders are typically for thousands of units, and they need to go to only one of three manufacturing centers: Austin, Ireland, and Malaysia. It's almost ideal from a supplier standpoint because we have real-time information on what the demand is, and all the supplier has to do is get the product to us.

***"If you have a 90-day lag between the point of demand and the point of supply, you're going to have a lot of inefficiency in the process."***

And because we build to our customers' order, typically, with just five or six days of lead time, suppliers don't have to worry about sell-through. We only maintain a few days—in some cases a few hours—of raw materials on hand. We communicate inventory levels and replenishment needs regularly—with some vendors, hourly.

The typical case in our industry is the factory building 10,000 units a day, day in and day out. First the machines stack up in the warehouse, and then they stack up in the channel. And all of a sudden, the guy at the end of the chain hollers, "Whoa, hey, we've got too many of these. Everybody stop!" And the order to stop flows back through the chain until it reaches every component supplier. It's literally stop and start, because if you have a 90-day lag between the point of demand and the point of supply, you're going to have a lot of inefficiency in the process. And the more inventory and time you have, the more variability, and the more problems.

In our industry, there's a lot of what I call bad hygiene. Companies stuff the channel to get rid of old inventory and to meet short-term financial objectives. We think our approach is better. We substitute information for inventory and ship only when we have real demand from real end customers.

***How does the direct model benefit your suppliers?***

We can go to Sony and say, "We're going to be pulling monitors from you in a very consistent, predictable way because the distance between the demand and the source of supply is totally shrunk." The longer that distance, the more intermediary channels you add, the less likely it is you will have good information about demand—so you will end up with more variability, more inventory, higher costs, and more risk.

Another factor that helps keep our demand for computers level is the mix of customers we serve. We don't have any customer that represents more than 1% to 2% of our revenues. One week Exxon is buying, the next week Shell is buying, the next week Ford is buying. But all companies don't decide in unison, "Well, this week we're going to buy, next week we're not."

***You mention your customer mix. Does the direct model imply a particular customer strategy?***

If you'd asked me that question 12 years ago, I would have said that we didn't differentiate much between our largest and our smallest customer. Today we do. Our customer strategy is one area where our model has evolved. We've become good at developing what we call "scalable" businesses—that is, those in which we can grow revenues faster than expenses. We really look closely at financial measures like gross margins by customer segment—and we focus on segments we can serve profitably as we achieve scale. People are sometimes surprised to learn that 90% of our sales go to institutions—business or government—and 70% to very large customers that buy at least $1 million in PCs per year.

When you're trying to target profitable segments, averages obscure a lot, and aggregate financial statements are pretty meaningless. Our approach to segmentation is to take really big numbers and "de-average" them. Until you look inside and understand what's going on by business, by customer, by geography, you don't know anything. This is a lesson we learned the hard way. We incorrectly entered the retail business in 1989, thinking that our direct business wouldn't grow enough, and went into computer superstores and warehouse clubs. But when we really started to understand the segment's profitability, we realized we'd made a mistake, and so we exited.

For years, we didn't actively pursue the consumer market because we couldn't reach our profit objectives. So we let our competitors introduce machines with rock-bottom prices and zero margins. We figured they could be the ones to teach consumers about PCs while we focused our efforts on more profitable segments. And then, because we're direct and can see who is buying what, we noticed something interesting. The industry's average selling price to consumers was going down, but ours was going up. Consumers who were now buying their second or third machines—who wanted the most powerful machines and needed less hand-holding—were coming to us. And without focusing on it in a significant way, we had a billion-dollar consumer business that was profitable. So we decided in 1997 that it was time to dedicate a group to serving that segment.

***So, over time, you cut the market into finer and finer segments?***

Yes, for a lot of reasons. One is to identify unique opportunities and economics. The other is purely a managerial issue: you can't possibly manage something well if it's too big. Segmentation gives us better attention and focus. [See the exhibit "Fast-Cycle Segmentation."]

Each segment has its own issues. In education, for instance, how do you get tech support to a classroom when the teacher doesn't have a telephone? You need a totally different approach. Segmenting lets you tailor your programs to the customers' needs. If you just lump diverse customers together, you can be sure that some of them will come last on some manager's list, and he may never get around to solving their problems. That's why we make serving one segment the manager's only job.

***"If our customers didn't work with us as partners, managing to 11 days of inventory would be insane."***

### Fast-Cycle Segmentation

*Dell's rapid growth in recent years has been accompanied by ever finer cuts at customer segmentation. This is an important element of Dell's virtual integration with customers. The finer the segmentation, the better able Dell is to forecast what its customers are going to need and when. Dell then coordinates the flow of that strategic information all the way back to its suppliers, effectively substituting information for inventory.*

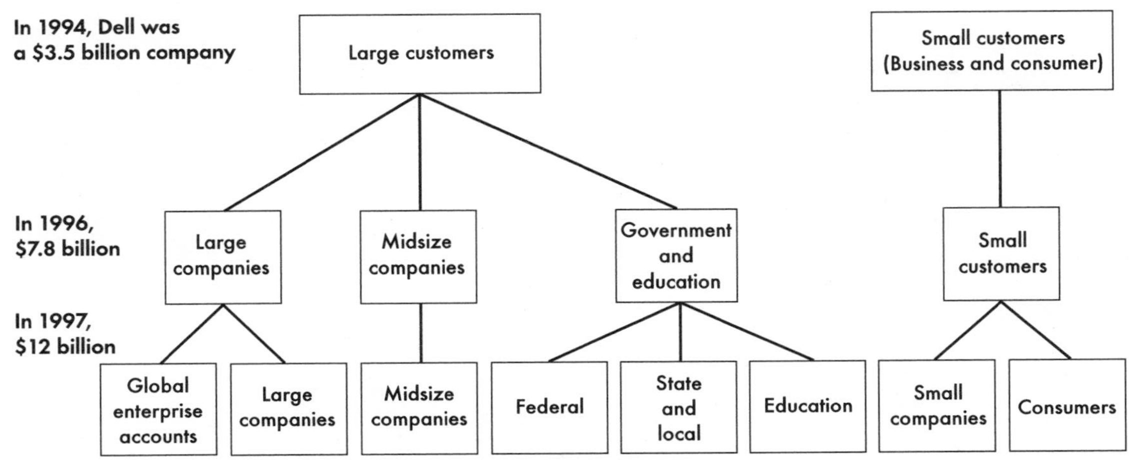

***Do you get other benefits from segmenting your customers?***

Segmentation gets us closer to them. It allows us to understand their needs in a really deep way. This closeness gives us access to information that's absolutely critical to our strategy. It helps us forecast what they're going to need and when. And good forecasts are the key to keeping our costs down.

We turn our inventory over 30 times per year. If you look at the complexity and the diversity of our product line, there's no way we could do that unless we had credible information about what the customer is actually buying. It's a key part of why rivals have had great difficulty competing with Dell. It's not just that we sell direct, it's also our ability to forecast demand—it's both the design of the product and the way the information from the customer flows all the way through manufacturing to our suppliers. If you don't have that tight linkage—the kind of coordination of information that used to be possible only in vertically integrated companies—then trying to manage to 11 days of inventory would be insane. We simply couldn't do it without customers who work with us as partners.

***Could you describe how you forecast demand?***

We see forecasting as a critical sales skill. We teach our sales-account managers to lead customers through a discussion of their future PC needs. We'll walk a customer through every department of his company, asking him to designate which needs are certain and which are contingent. And when they're contingent on some event, the salesperson will know what that event is so he can follow up. We can do this with our large accounts, which make up the bulk of our business. With smaller customers, we have real-time information about what they're buying from our direct telephone salespeople. And we can also steer them in real time, on the phone, toward configurations that are available, so this is another way we can fine-tune the balance between supply and demand.

***Is that what you mean by virtual integration with your customers?***

It's part of it. There are so many information links between us and our customers. For example, we can help large global customers manage their total purchase of PCs by selling them a standard product. Then when the guy whose computer isn't working calls in from Singapore, the IT people don't have to spend the first 30 minutes just figuring out what configuration of hardware and software he's using. Selling direct allows us to keep track of the company's total PC purchases, country by country—and that's valuable information we can feed back to them. We sometimes know more about a customer's operations than they do themselves.

Close customer relationships have allowed us to dramatically extend the value we deliver to our customers. Today we routinely load the customer's software in our factory. Eastman Chemical, for example, has their own unique mix of software, some of it licensed from Microsoft, some of it they've written themselves, some of it having to do with the way their network works. Normally, they would get their PCs, take them out of the box, and then some guy carrying a walkie-talkie and diskettes and CD-ROMs would come to each employee's desk to hook the system up and load all that software. Typically, this takes an hour or two—and costs $200 to $300—and it's a nuisance.

Our solution was to create a massive network in our factory with high-speed, 100-megabit Ethernet. We'll load Eastman Chemical's software onto a huge Dell server. Then when a machine comes down the assembly line and says, "I'm an Eastman Chemical analyst workstation, configuration number 14," all of a sudden a few hundred megabytes of data come rushing through the network and onto the workstation's hard disk, just as part of the progressive build through our factory. If the customer wants, we can put an asset tag with the company's logo on the machine, and we can keep an electronic register of the customer's assets. That's a lot easier than the customer sending some guy around on a thankless mission, placing asset tags on computers when he can find them.

What happens to the money our customer is saving? They get to keep most of it. We could say, "Well, it costs you $300 to do it, so we'll charge you $250." But instead we charge $15 or $20, and we make our product and our service much more valuable. It also means we're not going to be just your PC vendor anymore. We're going to be your IT department for PCs.

Boeing, for example, has 100,000 Dell PCs, and we have 30 people that live at Boeing, and if you look at the things we're doing for them or for other customers, we don't look like a supplier, we look more like Boeing's PC department. We become intimately involved in planning their PC needs and the configuration of their network.

It's not that we make these decisions by ourselves. They're certainly using their own people to get the best answer for the company. But the people working on PCs together, both from Dell and Boeing, understand the needs in a very intimate way. They're right there living it and breathing it, as opposed to the typical vendor who says, "Here are your computers. See you later."

We've always visited clients, but now some of our accounts are large enough to justify a dedicated on-site team. Remember, a lot of companies have far more complex problems to deal with than PC purchasing and servicing. They can't wait to get somebody else to take care of that so they can worry about more strategic issues.

***So some of your coordination with customers is made possible through technology, but there's still a good measure of old-fashioned, face-to-face human contact?***

Yes, that's right. The idea is to use technology to free people up to solve more complicated problems. For example, a customer like MCI can access our internal support tools on-line in the same way our own technical-support teams do, saving time and money on both sides. They simply go to www.dell.com, enter some information about their system, and they have immediate access to the same information that we use at Dell to help customers. These tools are used by internal help-desk groups at large companies as well as by individuals.

We've developed customized intranet sites called Premier Pages for well over 200 of our largest global customers. These exist securely within the customers' firewalls, and they give them direct access to purchasing and technical information about the specific configurations they buy from us. One of our customers, for example, allows its 50,000 employees to view and select products on-line. They use the Premier Page as an interactive catalog of all the configurations the company authorizes; employees can then price and order the PC they want.

They are happy to have some choice, and Dell and the customer are both happy to eliminate the paperwork and sales time normally associated with corporate purchasing. That frees our salespeople to play a more consultative role.

We also have developed tools to help customers set up their own customized versions of dell.com. There are about 7,000 of these to date.

***How else do you stay close to your customers?***

In a direct business like ours, you have, by definition, a relationship with customers. But beyond the mechanisms we have for sales and support, we have set up a number of forums to ensure the free flow of information with the customer on a constant basis. Our Platinum Councils, for example, are regional meetings—in Asia-Pacific, Japan, the United States, and Europe—of our largest customers. They meet every six to nine months; in the larger regions, there's one for the information executives—the CIO types—and then there's one for the technical types.

***"All our senior executives participate in these meetings with our largest customers. The ratio is about one Dell person to one customer."***

In these meetings, our senior technologists share their views on where the technology is heading and lay out road maps of product plans over the next two years. There are also breakout sessions and working groups in which our engineering teams focus on specific product areas and talk about how to solve problems that may not necessarily have anything to do with the commercial relationship with Dell. For example, Is leasing better than buying? or How do you manage the transition to

Windows NT? or How do you manage a field force of notebook computers?

People in businesses as dissimilar as Unilever and ICI can learn from each other because, amazingly, they have very similar problems when it comes to PCs. And we send not only our top technologists and engineers but also the real engineers, the people who usually don't get out to talk to customers because they're too busy developing products. All of our senior executives from around the company participate, spending time with the customer, listening to how we're doing. The ratio is about one Dell person to one customer. At our last session, we had about 100 customers.

The councils are another way we're able to play more of an advisory role, trying to help our customers understand what the flow of new technology really means, how it will translate into specific products. We try to help the customer anticipate what's happening and be ready. And that helps us, as well, with our own demand forecasting. So we're helping each other in important ways. We hire a lot of people from other companies in the industry, and they tell us that these meetings are unique.

***Do you spend a significant amount of your time at these meetings?***

I spend three days at each of them. They're great events. In the normal course of our business, I have lots of opportunity to talk to customers one on one, but there is something much more powerful about this kind of forum. Customers tend to speak more openly when they're with their peers and they know we're there and we're listening.

At every Platinum Council, we review what they told us last time and what we did about it. We keep an ongoing record of the issues. Let me give you a concrete example:

A few years ago, the engineers responsible for our desktops were operating on the theory that customers really wanted performance from these products—the faster the better. But what the customers actually said at the Platinum Councils was, "Yeah, performance, that's okay. But what I really want is a stable product that doesn't change. Because if I'm trying to run a bank or an airline, I don't care if it's 2% faster or 3% slower. What really matters is stability." So our engineers thought one thing, the customers thought another thing. It took the direct feedback from the Platinum Councils to spotlight this failure to communicate. We responded by building product with intergenerational consistency over many years. The same feedback has helped shape the creation of our brands. For both our desktop and notebook businesses, we created different brands designed to deliver greater stability to corporate customers, as opposed to the fast technology changes that consumers demand. (See "Using Information to Speed Execution" at the end of this article.)

***"Things that seem fairly small at the time have turned out three or four years later to be the basis for billions of dollars of revenue."***

As I think back to some of those council meetings, things that would seem fairly small at the time have often turned out three or four years later to become the basis for billions of dollars of revenue—notebooks with longer-life batteries, for example, or loading customers' software for them in our plants.

***As your customer strategy has evolved, has the Dell brand changed as well?***

A big piece of our brand is being the most efficient and effective way for customers to buy Intel or Microsoft technologies. But beyond that, we're evolving into a technology selector, or navigator. We often talk to customers about "relevant technology." Intel and Microsoft tend to launch into a massive variety of things, some of which are speculative and aimed at exploring new technologies. We think it's our job to help our customers sort out the technology relevant to today's needs from the bleeding edge.

***How does that strategy affect your own R&D function? What role does R&D play in your company?***

At Dell, we believe the customer is in control, and our job is to take all the technology that's out there and apply it in a useful way to meet the customer's needs. We're not trying to invent new architecture ourselves, but we'll spend a quarter of a billion dollars this year and employ some 1,500 people to improve the whole user experience—that means delivering the latest relevant technology, making it easy to use, and keeping costs down. And in addition to selecting appropriate technology, our R&D group focuses on process and quality improvements in manufacturing.

Before industry standards came into play, the proprietary computing environment bred a kind of technical arrogance that, fortunately, won't fly anymore. Once standards were established, the customer started to define what was going to be successful, and it didn't matter what you invented or how good it was or how fast it was. Increasingly, what matters is what the customers want and whether it works with all their other stuff.

That means we have to stay on top of our customers' needs, and we have to monitor and understand the innovations in the material science world—everything from semiconductors to polymers to liquid crystal displays. You need to track anything having to do with the flow of electrons, and you need to keep asking how these marvelous developments might be useful to customers. The customer doesn't come to you and say, "Boy, I really like lithium ion batteries. I can't wait to get my hands on some lithium ion." The customer says, "I want a notebook computer that lasts the whole day. I don't want it to run out when I'm on the plane."

I was about to leave a meeting at Sony in Tokyo in January of 1993 when someone ran up to me and said, "Oh, Mr. Dell, please wait one minute. I'm from Sony's power technology company. We have a new power-system technology we want to explain to you." And I remember thinking, Is this guy going to try to sell me a power plant? He starts showing me chart after chart about the performance of lithium ion batteries. This is wonderful, I tell him. And if it's true, we're going to put this in every notebook computer we make.

We then sent a team over to check it out, and a year and a half later we were the first computer company to have a notebook that lasted five-and-a-half, six hours. We tested it with American Airlines, handing out the notebooks to passengers at the start of flights from New York to Los Angeles. By the end, the notebooks were still running.

***How are the challenges of leadership in a virtually integrated organization different from those you would encounter running a corporation with more traditional boundaries?***

The whole idea behind virtual integration is that it lets you meet customers' needs faster and more efficiently than any other model. (See the exhibit "The Evolution of a Faster Business Model.") With vertical integration, you can be an efficient producer—as long as the world isn't changing very much. But virtual integration lets you be efficient and responsive to change at the same time—at least, that's what we're trying to do. We think about Internet commerce as a logical extension of our direct model—and within our first year, we reached a run rate of $2 million a day. It's now about $3 million a day, and during the peak of the Christmas buying season we saw several $6 million days. I'm only half joking when I say that the only thing better than the Internet would be mental telepathy. Because what we're all about is

---

### *The Evolution of a Faster Business Model*

**The dominant model in the personal computer industry**—a value chain with arms-length transactions from one layer to the next:

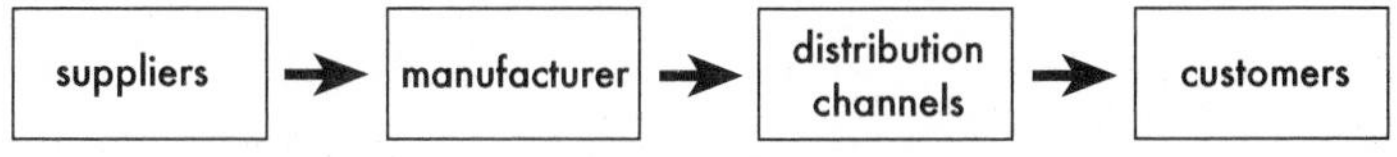


**Dell's direct model** eliminates the time and cost of third-party distribution:

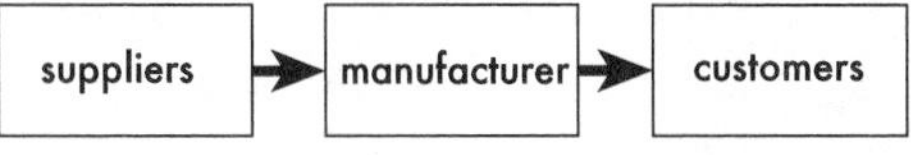


**Virtual integration** works even faster by blurring the traditional boundaries and roles in the value chain:

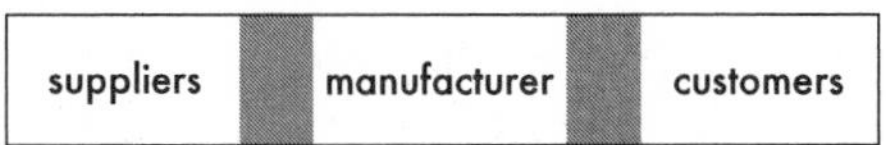

shrinking the time and the resources it takes to meet customers' needs. And we're trying to do that in a world where those needs are changing.

To lead in that kind of environment, you have to be on the lookout for shifts in value, and if the customer decides, "Hey, I don't care about that anymore, now I care about this," we may have to develop new capabilities rather quickly. One of the biggest challenges we face today is finding managers who can sense and respond to rapid shifts, people who can process new information very quickly and make decisions in real time. It's a problem for the computer industry as a whole—and not just for Dell—that the industry's growth has outpaced its ability to create managers. We tell prospective hires, "If you want an environment that is never going to change, don't come here. This is not the place for you."

Our goal is to be one or two steps ahead of the change, and in fact to be creating or shaping it, to some extent. That's why we spend so much time with our customers. It's why I personally spend about 40% of my time with customers. Often it's a lead customer that says, "Hey, can you put an asset tag on my PC?" And the first reaction is, "Gee, we've never done that before, but why not? Let's give it a try." And then you do it for one customer, then for ten, then for a hundred, and eventually it becomes a standard offering. Putting asset tags on computers isn't by itself a major value shift, but what happens is that we get a series of seemingly small innovations that over time add up to a huge improvement. That's not a bad description of the way we get into businesses. We don't come at it the other way around, with a consulting study that says, "That's an attractive business. Let's go." Nor do we sit around and say, "What do we suppose our customers would like? If we were customers, what would we be thinking?"

So looking for value shifts is probably the most important dimension of leadership. Then there's the question of managing such a tightly coordinated value chain—and there it's all about execution. If you look at Dell's P&L structure, I think you'd be hard-pressed to find companies that deliver the kind of value-added we do with such a small markup. My theory is that if we can continue to keep our markup as low as it is today, we're going to be able to capture most of the opportunities available to us. But that means we cannot get complacent about our growth and get careless about execution.

Sometimes, I'm taken aback when I talk to people who've been in the company for six months or a year and who talk about "the model" as if it were an all-powerful being that will take care of everything. It's scary because I know that nothing is ever 100% constant, and the last thing we should do is assume that we're always going to be doing well. But for now, it's working. The direct system really delivers value to the customer all the way from distribution back through manufacturing and design. If you tried to divide Dell up into a manufacturer and a channel, you'd destroy the company's unique value. It's something completely new that nobody in our industry has ever done before.

---

## Using Information to Speed Execution

***by Kevin Rollins***

MOST OF THE MANAGERIAL challenges at Dell Computer have to do with what we call *velocity*—speeding the pace of every element of our business. Life cycles in our business are measured in months, not years, and if you don't move fast, you're out of the game. Managing velocity is about managing information–using a constant flow of information to drive operating practices, from the performance measures we track to how we work with our suppliers.

### Performance Metrics

At Dell, we use the balance sheet and the fundamentals of the P&L on a monthly basis as tools to manage operations. From the balance sheet, we track three cash-flow measures very closely. We look at weekly updates of how many days of inventory we have, broken out by product component. We can then work closely with our suppliers so we end up with the right inventory. When it's not quite right, we can use our direct-sales model to steer customers toward comparable products that we do have. So we use inventory information to work both the front and back ends at the same time.

We also track and manage receivables and payables very tightly. This is basic blocking and tackling, but we give it a high priority. The payoff is that we have a negative cash-conversion cycle of five days–that is, we get paid before we have to pay our suppliers. Since our competitors usually have to support their resellers by offering them credit, the direct model gives us an inherent cost advantage. And the more we can shorten our cash-collection cycle, the greater our advantage.

The real-time performance measures in the P&L that we regard as the best indicators of the company's health are our margins, our average selling price, and the overhead associated with selling. We split the P&L into these core elements by customer segment, by product, and by country. These metrics can alert us instantly to problems, for example, with the mix of products being sold in any particular country.

## Working with Suppliers

The greatest challenge in working with suppliers is getting them in sync with the fast pace we have to maintain. The key to making it work is information. The right information flows allow us to work with our partners in ways that enhance speed, either directly by improving logistics or indirectly by improving quality.

Take our service strategy, for example. Customers pay us for service and support, and we contract with third-party maintainers (TPMs) to make the service calls. Customers call us when they have problems, and that initial call will trigger two electronic dispatches–one to ship the needed parts directly from Dell to the customers' sites and one to dispatch the TPMs to the customers. Our role as information broker facilitates the TPMs' work by making sure the necessary parts will be on-site when they arrive.

But our role doesn't stop there. Because poor quality creates friction in the system, which slows us down, we want to capture information that can be used to fix problems so they won't happen again. So we take back the bad part to diagnose what went wrong, and we feed that information back to our suppliers so they can redesign the component. Clearly, we couldn't operate that way if we were dealing with hundreds of suppliers. So for us, working with a handful of partners is one of the keys to improving quality–and therefore speed–in our system.

**Kevin Rollins** *is vice chairman of Dell Computer Corporation.*

**Originally published in March–April 1998**
**Reprint 98208**

# Competing on Customer Service

## *An Interview with British Airways' Sir Colin Marshall*

STEVEN E. PROKESCH

## Executive Summary

JUST BECAUSE THE COMPETITION is tough, that's no reason to be tough on customers, says Sir Colin Marshall, chairman of British Airways. Even in a cutthroat, mass-market business such as air travel, he argues, many people will pay a premium for good service–even those who travel economy. Marshall's view may be unconventional, but so is his company's performance: While the world airline industry has racked up billions of dollars in losses, British Airways has remained solidly profitable.

Under his leadership, British Airways has striven to go beyond providing the basics (flying people from point A to point B on time, safely, and at the lowest cost). It has striven to provide customers with a high-quality, highly personal *experience*. Creating a service with "a global scope but a homey feel," as Marshall puts it, is no easy feat in a business where dozens of human interactions shape each customer's experience. But besides being hard for competitors to copy, this capability will help British Airways minimize customer churn and maximize its share of each customer's business, Marshall insists.

In "Championing the Customer," British Airways manager Charles R. Weiser describes the lead role that the airline's customer relations department plays in reducing customer defections. It encourages customers to report their problems, strives to make quick amends when service failures occur, and helps spot and eliminate operational weaknesses that cause service failures. The approach has attracted new customers, reduced the cost of retaining customers, and helped increase the airline's share of customers' business.

---

*Few businesses are as brutally competitive as airlines. But just because the competition is tough, that's no reason to be tough on customers, says Sir Colin Marshall, the chairman of British Airways. Convinced that travelers care mainly about price, many airlines–most notably the major U. S. carriers–seem to have made cutting costs the top priority at the expense of their service quality. But Marshall doesn't think it has to be that way. Even in a cutthroat, mass-market business such as air travel, he argues, there are plenty of people who will pay a premium for good service–even among those who travel economy. It may sound crazy, but just look at British Airways' profits: While the world airline industry has racked up billions of dollars in losses in the last five years, British Airways has remained solidly profitable.*

*With his talk of building brand equity and commanding a premium by "orchestrating service to fill customers' value-driven needs," Marshall, who is 61 years old, is clearly an iconoclast in the airline industry. Then again, he is not a product of the industry. His first job was as a ship's purser. He then worked all over the world as a manager for Hertz and later Avis, where he became CEO in 1976. After the conglomerate Norton Simon acquired Avis in 1979, Marshall's responsibilities expanded to include Hunt-Wesson foods, which instilled in him an appreciation for the power of brands. Sears, the British retailer and shoe manufacturer, lured him back to London in 1981 by offering him the deputy CEO's job. Then in 1983, John King came calling. Appointed by Margaret Thatcher, the industrialist was in the midst of his struggle to turn loss-ridden, state-owned British Airways into a competitive airline that investors might want to own.*

*Together, King and Marshall transformed the airline, which they privatized in 1987. Marshall, who joined British Airways as CEO and succeeded King as chairman in 1993, has presided over British Airways' metamorphosis from a company that seemed to disdain customers to one that strives to please them. Although Marshall certainly isn't yet proclaiming victory on that front, a much larger challenge is now looming. In a bid to become the first truly global airline, British Airways has been forging alliances with other carriers around the world. It has taken sizable stakes in USAir, Australia's Qantas Airways, France's TAT European Airlines, and Deutsche BA. If delivering consistent, high-quality service in a complex people business is tremendously difficult for one company, think about trying to get a group of companies to do it. From his offices in London, Marshall talked with HBR senior editor Steven E. Prokesch about competing in service industries.*

---

***How can a large competitor such as British Airways differentiate itself in a commodity services business that is so cutthroat?***

You're always going to be faced with the fact that the great majority of people will buy on price. But even for a seeming commodity such as air travel, an element of the traveling public is willing to pay a slight premium for superior service. They are the people we've been trying to attract and retain as customers. We don't just mean people who fly business class, first class, or the Concorde. Many service companies ignore the fact that there also are plenty of customers in the lower end of the market who are willing to pay a little more for superior service.

***"Many service companies ignore the fact that there also are plenty of customers in the lower end of the market who are willing to pay a little more for superior service."***

It all comes back in the end to value for money. If you can deliver something extra that others are not or cannot, some people will pay a slight premium for it. I want to stress that when I say "slight," I mean precisely that. In our case, we're talking about an average of 5%. On our revenues of £5 billion, however, that 5% translates into an extra £250 million, or $400 million, a year.

It's true that we can't command a premium everywhere, but we've succeeded in most of our international markets, including the majority of routes between

Britain and the East Coast of the United States. That's why our profits from and share of that market have continued to climb in recent years despite the tough competition on routes such as the one between London's Heathrow airport and New York's John F. Kennedy airport, and despite growing competition from strong companies such as American, United, and Virgin Atlantic.

***In industry after industry, companies seem to be competing mainly on cost and price. That certainly seems to be the case in the U.S. airline industry. What do you think of this approach?***

I think it is flawed. Most of the major U.S. airlines have not been very innovative or creative. Compared with international flying anyway, the flying experience in the United States today is pretty ghastly. We've conducted extensive research with USAir and have very strong indications that many people in the United States are willing to pay a premium not to be treated like cattle. They want to be respected and rewarded for their business—and not just with frequent-flier miles, which have become a commodity, a price of entry into the market. We think we—through USAir—could revolutionize the U.S. airline industry and create an entirely new section of the industry. USAir is beginning to implement this strategy with its new Business Select service.

There are two sides to the business equation: costs and revenues. Any business that focuses on one at the expense of the other is going to pay very heavily. You can't walk away from the fact that if somebody can do the job better and cheaper, you have a problem and you have to do something about it. But you can do it without undermining the fabric of what you have built up. When business conditions got tough in recent years, we did not take meat cleavers to our product. We did not reduce costs indiscriminately. We did not reduce the quality of the wine. We did not stop investing in airport lounges and in training people. We continued making that investment despite the fact that it would have been very easy not to. Why is it that people prefer to fly business class with us? It's because our product is better.

There are different ways to think about how to compete in a mass-market service business such as ours. One is to think that a business is merely performing a function—in our case, transporting people from point A to point B on time and at the lowest possible price. That's the commodity mind-set, thinking of an airline as the bus of the skies. Another way to compete is to go beyond the function and compete on the basis of providing an experience. In our case, we want to make the process of flying from point A to point B as effortless and pleasant as possible. Anyone can fly airplanes, but few organizations can excel in serving people. Because it's a competence that's hard to build, it's also hard for competitors to copy or match.

To use a rather overdone term, we decided that our goal should be to make our service more seamless than our competitors'. By that I mean we aim to remove some of the common hassles that one encounters when traveling today, thereby making the customer's whole experience easier. For instance, we have worked with British government authorities to install fast-track channels at Heathrow and Gatwick airports to make it easier for our premium, or full-fare, passengers to speed through immigration and customs. And unlike many U.S. airlines, which charge people for access to their lounges, our lounges are part of our products. Access is included in our Concorde, First Class, Club World (intercontinental business class), and Club Europe (European business class) products and is a reward for our top frequent fliers. Everything in our lounges—from drinks to telephone service—is free.

There's another critical element of our approach to serving customers: Filling customers' value-driven needs. Every industry has a price of entry—the ante you have to pay to get into the game. In our industry, there are five basic services that everyone has to provide. We must: get passengers to where they want to go, do it safely, go when they want to go, provide some nourishment, and let them accrue frequent-flier miles. But our research shows that customers now take the basics for granted and increasingly want a company to desire to help them, to treat them in a personal, caring way. Fulfilling those desires is the centerpiece of how we wish to orchestrate our service.

***What do you mean by orchestrating service?***

I mean exactly that: arranging all the elements of our service so that they collectively generate a particular experience. We try to think about what kind of impression or feeling each interaction between the company and a customer will generate. For instance, we ask our crews not to load up passengers with food and drinks and then disappear—not for cost reasons but so we can create additional personal contacts with the customer. According to our research, just seeing crew members creates higher customer-satisfaction levels. Other airlines pile on the food and drinks so that their crew members don't have to go back.

I mentioned that we strive to make our customers' travel experience seamless, personal, and caring. We continually ask customers in focus groups to tell us what such an experience should look and feel like, and we have distilled their responses into service principles that are enshrined in two of our corporate goals. The goals are: "To provide overall superior service and good value for money in every market segment in which we compete" and "to excel in anticipating and quickly responding to customer needs and competitor activity." These corporate goals have, in turn, been incorporated into our customer service department's mission statement: "To ensure that British Airways is the customer's first choice through the delivery of an unbeatable travel experience."

We want to create an airline with a global scope but a homey feel. The phrase "nothing too small, nothing too big" captures what we're trying to achieve. The "nothing too big" or global image, our customers have told us, lets them know that we go where they're going and that we're professional. The "nothing too small" feeling lets them know that we have orchestrated our services to look after their individual needs. We want them to know that we carry millions but to feel that our individual interactions with them weren't mass produced. The theme of our latest worldwide advertising campaign is: "It's how we make you feel which makes us the world's favorite airline."

***Could you provide a concrete illustration of a service you created in order to fill customers' value-driven needs?***

When we found that many long-haul travelers felt poorly when they arrived at their destinations, we began our Well-Being in the Air program to help passengers combat fatigue and improve their circulation. It consists of healthful meal choices and a video demonstrating exercises that customers can perform in their seats. That's relatively small. But we also designed a whole new service—our Sleeper Service—for First Class customers flying long routes: They can eat a real dinner in the lounge before boarding and change into "sleeper suits" (pajamas) on the plane. Upon arriving in Britain, they can use our arrivals lounges, which are a major innovation. They're places where our First Class and Club World customers can get messages left overnight while they were in the air; have breakfast; read a newspaper; shower; get a manicure, haircut, or shave; have clothes pressed; and then catch a taxi or subway or train into town. We maintain full arrival-lounge facilities at Heathrow and Gatwick, our prime network-hub airports; and at Birmingham, Glasgow, and Manchester airports we offer similar complimentary comforts at hotels adjacent to the airport terminals.

Many passengers arriving on long overnight flights need a place to go when their flights get in very early—before public transport or offices are open. Our research revealed that they thought that airlines, including British Airways, took their money and dumped them without a care. In other words, we were not filling a value-driven need.

Our main arrivals lounges at the London airports are used by an average of around 200 customers each day. They unquestionably played a significant part in boosting our premium business by 9% during our last fiscal year, which ended March 31. The Sleeper Service has been similarly well received. Since its introduction in February 1995, First Class bookings between New York and London, for instance, have increased by as much as 25%. To varying extents, competitors are copying these initiatives, but British Airways enjoys the halo effect that comes from being first.

Not all potential customers will care about or value our approach to service. But even in a mass-market business, you don't want to attract and retain everyone. As far as we're concerned, the key is first to identify and attract those who will value your service and then to retain them as customers and win the largest possible share of their lifetime business. We know that 35% of our customers account for more than 60% of our sales. Using database-marketing techniques, we have focused more of our marketing effort on retaining those customers and increasing our share of their business. That's why our advertising spending is proportionately smaller than that of our competitors.

Although other companies employ similar marketing techniques, we think ours are pretty sophisticated. First, we extensively and continuously study the market to pinpoint the segments that offer the possibility of generating a higher profit margin—segments such as business women, unaccompanied minors, and consultants—and identify those people among our customers. Then we create extensive lifestyle profiles of each customer, which we use both to increase ticket purchases and to sell other products and services. In addition to tracking how recently and how frequently customers have flown with us for business and for leisure, we track their broader purchasing behavior, lifestyles, their ability to influence other people's purchasing decisions, and their value needs. But identifying such customers is only half the battle. Learning from them so you can design and improve services that they will highly value over time is the other half. That's where we think we especially excel.

***Competing by delivering an experience, by filling customers' value-driven needs as you put it, must be***

***extremely difficult in a service business. Presumably, it's much easier to achieve a consistent standard in consumer packaged goods because it's much easier to create a formula that gets a product to perform in a particular way and then to manufacture that product consistently.***

You're absolutely right. With packaged goods, you can pull something off the line to test it periodically, and adjust it if there's something wrong. A packaged-goods business has the most incredible market data available to it. It knows how it's performing by store, even by positioning on the shelves in the store. That kind of reliable information is just not available in our industry or in service businesses generally because a service business is dealing with people's impressions and feelings. They don't actually buy an object; they buy an experience.

In addition, so many human interactions are involved in producing an experience in a service business that it is often difficult to measure which interaction or series of interactions caused a customer to feel satisfied or dissatisfied. On top of that, a customer may have a bad experience because of circumstances outside our control—a flight delay caused by bad weather, for example, or problems with air-traffic control. As a result, it is often difficult to know if a complaint is the result of an isolated event—perhaps one crew just having a bad day–or a systemic problem.

***How can a service company overcome such formidable obstacles?***

By creating an organization that excels in listening to its most valuable customers. By creating data that enable you to measure the kinds of performance that create value for those customers so you can improve performance and spot and correct any weaknesses. And by recognizing that the people on the front line are the ones who ultimately create value since they are the ones who determine the kinds of experiences that the company generates for its customers. We focus intensively on the customer, and our marketing, our operating philosophy, and our performance measures reflect that.

In several key places in our organization, we have created customer advocates: in our brand-management organization; in our marketplace performance unit, which is responsible for benchmarking our operations and collecting data; and in our customer relations department.

I guess the importance of brand management came home to me during my Norton Simon days, when I was responsible for Hunt-Wesson. That experience shaped the way I perceive service products. It helped me realize that instilling a brand culture is very important in a service business because a service business is all about serving people, who have values, ideals, and feelings. It helped me realize that we needed to see the product not simply as a seat but more comprehensively as an experience being orchestrated across the airline. That orchestration was the brand.

BA's seven brand managers are customers' main advocates within BA. They oversee the process of refreshing the brands and are among those responsible for thinking of ways to innovate and improve services. Each of our services—Concorde, First Class, Club Europe, Club World, Euro Traveller (European economy), World Traveller (long-haul economy), and domestic Shuttle service—has its own brand manager. We started to treat our categories of service as brands in the mid-1980s. We came to recognize that there is a wear-out factor in terms of the way we present our different categories or classes of service just as there's a wear-out factor for consumer products and their branding approach.

We recognized that delivering consistent exceptional service was not enough—that service brands, like packaged-goods brands, need to be periodically refreshed to reinforce the message that the customer is receiving superior value for the money. Refreshing your service is also a way to make sure you periodically reassess how the value you think you are delivering compares with the value customers think you are delivering. When we began, I thought the wear-out factor for a service brand was somewhere in the five-year range. Now I am pretty convinced that five years is about the maximum that you can go without refreshing the brand.

***How does refreshing a service brand differ from refreshing a packaged-goods brand?***

For consumer products, refreshing the brand may only require different labeling. But refreshing a service brand so the customer will really recognize the change requires something major. It can't be something superficial such as changing the color of the menus.

For example, when we relaunched our Club Europe service recently, we added some of the best short-haul cuisine anywhere in the world (to meet the needs of the numerous culinary cultures across Europe) and added nine new airport lounges throughout Europe. In addition, we created the most ergonomic short-haul seat around, a telephone check-in service, and a valet-parking service. Competitive pressure didn't force us to do this. We did it because we wanted to stay ahead so that we could continue to win premium customers.

Refreshing a brand also might mean a complete revamp of in-flight entertainment. For example, when we refreshed our World Traveller, or economy class, brand last year, we completely overhauled the audio and video channels. We are currently creating interactive video services for our new Boeing 777s. Customers will be able to complain to our customer relations department in-flight, order duty-free goods, gamble, get the latest news on business, fashion, and so forth. World Traveller's markets are, in general, very price-sensitive, but again, we're hoping to attract a greater portion of economy fliers who are willing to pay for value, which incidentally is one reason we don't reward frequent fliers with upgrades.

It always amazes us how U.S. airlines undermine the integrity of their products with upgrades. We have invested millions to research, develop, and deliver products to serve particular market segments and to build up brand equity. We need to get a healthy return on that investment so we can continue to reinvest. We also don't wish to alienate those customers who choose to pay for First Class or Club by degrading the brand. Conversely, upgrading people out of World Traveller would not add value to that service and would detract from our ability to focus on the needs of those customers, which are very different from the needs of those who travel Club. Upgrading people out of economy shouldn't be seen as relief. If getting an upgrade is the only way a customer feels he or she can get value, then our World Traveller brand is not doing its job, and we will have long-term commodity problems like our U.S. counterparts.

I've digressed. There's one additional large benefit that we reap by refreshing our brands: It motivates our employees. They see that management is genuinely committed to delivering high-quality service. Our employees want to be proud of their product and they want to feel that they are making a difference to customers. When competitors surpass our product, and especially when customers tell them so, our employees become upset. They are very vocal in letting management know about such situations. They really are committed to delivering quality. They want to be part of a winning team.

***British Airways has a reputation for listening to customers more effectively than many other airlines. How do you listen?***

Of course, we do many things that lots of companies do. Our senior managers, myself included, consciously try to talk to a lot of our passengers when we fly and move around London and the world at large. We also conduct customer forums to help us continually improve our current products and services and to help us identify services that we should consider developing over the longer term. In these forums, we ask customers to let their imagination, anger, enthusiasm, and ideas flow so we can capture their thoughts about current as well as emergent issues. But we think we've gone far beyond other companies—at least other companies in our industry—in developing additional methods for listening to customers. I'm specifically thinking of our market performance unit and our customer relations department.

Over the years, I have seen a lot of marketing people who had been very successful in the packaged-goods business fail in the service business because, as I said, it is so difficult to get reliable data. That's one of the first things I tackled when I joined British Airways. My attitude was, If the information does not exist, create it. So in 1983, we formed what we call our *marketplace performance unit.* The unit, which is charged with representing the customer's point of view, is completely separate from, and therefore independent of, the marketing, selling, and operating side of the business. Its role is to measure how we are doing relative to the standards we set for ourselves, relative to the way customers expect us to perform, and relative to competitors' performance. (See "Measuring Performance Through Customers' Eyes" at the end of this article.)

***"We have transformed customer relations from a defensive complaint department into a department of customer champions whose mission is to retain customers."***

We also are trying to learn from customers by tapping a source of information that many service companies do not exploit fully: customer complaints, suggestions, and compliments. We have transformed customer relations from a defensive complaint department into a department of customer champions whose mission is to retain customers. (See "Championing the Customer," by Charles R. Weiser, HBR November–December 1995.) Our goal is to make BA as approachable as possible and to respond to customers as quickly as possible, which again fits into our value-driven customer strategy. Both approachability and responsiveness strongly influence customer loyalty. I ardently believe that customer complaints are precious opportunities to hold on to customers who otherwise might take their business elsewhere and to learn about problems that need to be fixed. Customers who make the effort to register a complaint are doing you a favor because they are giving you an opportunity to retain them, if you act quickly.

***You mentioned that it is difficult to deliver a consistent experience in a service business because numerous interactions between individual employees and the customer shape the experience. You hinted that achieving such consistency can produce a significant advantage that will be hard for competitors to copy.***

Delivering long-term and consistent value in a service business begins and ends with the way employees are trained, nurtured, and led. We have a rigorous process for selecting new employees. It includes résumé screening, psychological testing, group exercises, and one-on-one interviews in which we probe areas of concern. Just as important is leadership; our managers are continually trained in leadership and in techniques to provide high-quality service. Finally, we have established performance criteria—we call them *key performance indicators*—that each team must fulfill. They are based on research on the level of performance we must achieve to remain efficient and to win repeat business. They ensure a focus on facts as opposed to personal perceptions. These practices may not sound unique, but we think we take them much more seriously than many companies do.

We strongly believe that to deliver consistent service quality, our employees must understand their role in delivering superior service and must have the power and ability to deal with customer problems. Teams must receive constant feedback on their service interactions.

Toward that end, we hand out survey cards to passengers on every flight, and every day we ask a random sample of passengers who have just finished their flights to comment on our service quality. The person in charge of the cabin crew, the customer service director, receives this information, as does the crew, and it is used to assess performance and to identify training needs.

***How do you get employees to understand and then deliver superior consistent service?***

By giving them the freedom to act within specified boundaries. I try to impress upon our people that in a service business the customer doesn't expect everything will go right all the time; the big test is what you do when things go wrong. If you react quickly and in the most positive way, you can get very high marks from the customer. Recovery matters as much as trying to provide good service, since occasional service failure is unavoidable in a business like ours.

***"The customer doesn't expect everything will go right all the time; the big test is what you do when things go wrong. . . . Occasional service failure is unavoidable."***

We want every employee who interacts with customers to listen to them and to be able to address issues that arise immediately. Consider the following incident: An aircraft door was left open in a rain-storm before takeoff, and a passenger near the door unfortunately got showered. The flight attendant not only did everything that was routine—offered to have the customer's garments cleaned or replaced and made sure that a customer relations representative contacted the customer later to demonstrate that we genuinely cared—but also made a special gesture by offering the passenger a complimentary choice of certain tax-free goods.

We try to make it clear to employees that we expect them to respond to customers on the spot—before a customer writes a letter or makes a phone call. It's an important focus in our training. We created a series of training programs on the importance of good customer service and how to provide it. My objective from the day we launched our initial program, Putting People First, at the end of 1983 was to give all our employees the opportunity to go through a motivational program on customer service at least once every three years. That may not sound very frequent, but given the size of our workforce, it was the best we could do because it takes us about $2^1/_2$ years to get all our employees through one. Responding to service failure was the focus of the most recent program, which was called Winning for Customers. The program's message was that employees have the freedom to act. But the program doesn't just tell them that, it puts them through a series of simulations and exercises that show them how they can help customers when problems occur.

***How does British Airways ensure that managers encourage employees to take the initiative in providing good service, including helping to resolve customers' problems?***

We realize that employees—all of us—won't always be right, but it is better that they make mistakes than not try to solve customers' problems. We discourage our managers from coming down on an employee like a ton of bricks if the decision the employee made was wrong. Instead, we want managers to explain why the decision was wrong and what the right decision would have been, so that the next time the employee is confronted with a similar situation, he or she will get it right.

We want our staff to know that management genuinely does care about the problems that our staff encounters. It is not an easy thing to achieve, but we keep hammering away at it. We're trying to reinforce that kind of management behavior constantly with our compensation and performance-measurement systems, with training (each of the customer-service programs had a parallel program for managers), and with a 360-degree feedback program we're now installing, which will provide feedback to managers from subordinates, peers, and superiors. Managers who are merely paying lip service to supporting subordinates will have nowhere to hide.

Last but certainly not least, our senior managers demonstrate their commitment to looking after the customer. At many companies, senior managers say it's very important to look after the customer but don't demonstrate their commitment when they're interacting with customers and their own people. I'd like to think we're different. We strive to practice visible management. When we put everyone through the original Putting People First program, I tried to take questions at the end of as many sessions as I could. If I couldn't make it, another senior manager closed the session and reported back to me about any big issues that came up. That's a practice we continued with the other programs in the series. In addition, we expect senior managers to attend the customer-listening forums regularly, to take calls or at least listen in on calls that come into the customer relations department's Care Line, and to discuss with our customer relations people the causes of and possible solutions to customer-service issues.

I also should mention profit sharing. One of the first things I did when I joined the company was introduce a profit sharing program. In the United States, such programs may be common, but they were quite alien in the United Kingdom at the time. We want our employees to understand that there is a direct connection between the service we deliver and the profits we earn. There have been 2 years in the past 12 when the program hasn't paid out because the profits weren't high enough. Those were the year of and the year following the Gulf War. In our financial year that ended this past March 31, we achieved record earnings, and every eligible employee received a profit-share bonus equivalent to just over three weeks' pay.

***You have had a wide-ranging career. How did you come to hold your views on the importance of customer service?***

To differing degrees, all the businesses I have worked in have been service businesses—or people businesses, as I like to call them. When I became a Norton Simon executive after it bought Avis, I still had overall responsibility for Avis as well as for Hunt-Wesson foods and a couple of other smaller subsidiaries. And Sears also had a service business—its retail stores. All those experiences have been invaluable in helping me to develop an awareness of the importance of the interrelationship between employees, customers, and shareholders. Employees need to understand why shareholder return is important, and shareholders need to understand the necessity of investments that produce a long-term payback. Customers must understand that in order to satisfy their needs ever more effectively, we need to have an enduring relationship with them.

Some people wonder how a company can not only contemplate but actually implement and maintain extensive training, motivation, and incentive programs such as ours. My response is that for a service business, they are not decorative embroideries but essential parts of the company fabric. From the customer's perspective, the quality and value of the product are determined to a great extent by the people delivering the service. We therefore have to "design" our people and their service attitude, just as we design an aircraft seat, an in-flight entertainment program, or an airport lounge to meet the needs and preferences of our customers.

I suppose my evangelistic determination to strive for customer-service excellence goes back to my career beginnings as a cadet purser with the former Orient Line shipping company. One day on a long voyage between Europe and Australia was much the same as another for passengers and crew alike. The trick, however, was to ensure that each day was like the first day at sea, with product polish and service sparkle at its brightest all the time. That way, both customers and staff derived a sense of real value. My philosophy evolved further in the intensely competitive car-rental business, where the automobiles are very similar if not exactly the same and the initial transaction and the after-sale service are what make the difference.

I have to say that working in the discerning U.S. consumer market for many years was an invaluable experience. It helped bring home to me the importance of emphasizing customer-service excellence in business strategy.

***How do your extensive efforts to build a global network through alliances with other airlines mesh with your***

***vision of what it takes to prevail in a service business such as yours?***

In ten years' time, our industry will be much larger—probably twice its current size in terms of total traffic on a global basis. Clearly some markets, especially those in the Far East and Eastern Europe, will be growing much faster than the long-established markets of North America and Western Europe. And two other likely developments should lead to lower fares, thereby fueling worldwide demand: global deregulation and the introduction of an aircraft with a much larger carrying capacity and lower operating costs than the 747.

We don't think that the number of airlines will grow significantly, however. On the contrary, we think that deregulation will lead to consolidation. It is already happening, although it remains to be seen whether the consolidation of the global industry will be as drastic as the consolidation that occurred after the U.S. market was deregulated. We fully intend not just to survive but to be one of the major players, and the global network we are building is an integral part of our strategy. We are betting that this network will enable us to lower our costs. We will be able to share resources such as airport terminals and information systems, to buy and use aircraft more efficiently, and to use employees more efficiently. We also are betting that the network will increase our collective share of the world market, and that it will generate more business for our partners than they would be able to obtain on their own.

***How do you maintain consistent levels of service throughout your network so that a customer identifies a partner's service with your brand? Conversely, how***

***do you make sure that inconsistent service across the network does not undermine your—British Airways'—brand?***

I don't rule out our having a common name eventually, but that's a long way off. We wouldn't want to get rid of the individual names unless market research told us that it would benefit both the individual companies and the partnership as a whole.

In addition, there are different service expectations in different marketplaces. For example, business class, which falls between first class and economy, is the preeminent service on our international routes and our short-haul routes in Europe, but it is only beginning to emerge in the U.S. domestic market. The key is to make sure that even if each partner's service is different, it has the look and feel of a high-quality, value-driven product.

In situations where one partner is starting a service from scratch that another, say British Airways, already offers, we will at least explore whether it makes sense to make the partner's service similar to the one already established. For example, we did this with USAir when we helped it redesign its business-class service.

But overall, our aim for the network at this point is twofold: to create seamless service and to create a common public identity in the market over time without adopting a single name. We believe we can create a common identity through frequent-flier programs and by sharing frequent-flier lounges—steps we have already taken. Perhaps over time we will be able to move toward the adoption of a similar uniform and logo styles. By "creating seamless service" I mean dovetailing our route networks and our flight schedules, sharing codes to make it easier for customers to book a trip that involves legs flown with two or more of us, and making it easier and more pleasant to transfer between partners.

With our partners, we're beginning to work our way through these things. Our marketplace performance unit now tracks how our partners perform, so we have the data we need to compare services and decide where changes are in order. We also are working on a joint approach to information technology, which should provide the underpinning for a greater uniformity of customer service. For example, Qantas is switching over to BABS, British Airways' reservation system; USAir and BA are combining their frequent-flier databases; and we're exploring taking similar steps with TAT and Deutsche BA. This technology integration will allow us to share information on customers and costs, which will then allow partners in the network to take a network perspective when they make decisions about investments ranging from aircraft purchases to catering.

***When you have an alliance, with whom is the employee supposed to identify?***

It's very important, at least in these early years, that employees clearly identify with the company for which they work. It is also important that they recognize the existence of the alliance, see it as a good thing, and talk about it in a positive way.

I hope that, over time, we shall be able to engage in a larger degree of employee exchange. In fact, we already have some. For example, some of British Airways' North Atlantic routes have been flown by leased USAir aircraft painted in our livery, and operated by USAir pilots and cabin staff wearing our uniforms and delivering the authentic British Airways product. Obviously, this has meant teaching the USAir employees British Airways' methods and training them to perform to our standards; it also has required a great deal of interairline cooperation. The arrangement has been very successful as far as the customer is concerned—and tremendously mind-expanding for us.

***What is the alliance's overarching objective?***

It is the development of an integrated global air-transport system in which consistency of product, service standards, and operational integrity is implicit throughout. Our multinational combine will be able to be at the forefront of technological development, whether in the introduction of new large aircraft to succeed the existing jumbo jets or in the implementation of advanced ground-handling systems that will render the check-in queue, the delays in clearing immigration and customs, and the unseemly scramble for baggage upon arrival things of the past.

There is immense scope for invention, innovation, and pushing out the competitive frontier. Not the least exciting aspect of the future will be that as staff become freed from the existing mechanical humdrum of air-travel procedures, a whole new dimension in personal customer service will open up. For me, this, more than the application of new technology, forms the great challenge of the future.

---

## Measuring Performance Through Customers' Eyes

MANY SERVICE BUSINESSES suffer from a problem: the lack of comparative data to measure and benchmark operating performance. "If the information doesn't exist, create it," says Sir Colin Marshall, British Airways' chairman. That is exactly what Marshall set out to do when he created his company's *marketplace performance unit* in 1983.

The 10-member unit tracks some 350 measures of performance, including aircraft cleanliness, punctuality, technical defects on aircraft, customers' opinions on British Airways' check-in performance, the time it takes for a customer to get through when telephoning a reservations agent, customer satisfaction with in-flight and ground services, and the number of involuntary downgrades that have occurred in a given time period. It issues a monthly report, which goes to the chairman, the managing director, the CFO, and the top management team responsible for service and performance. Besides reporting on the *key performance indicators* (key operating data), the report typically has a section that focuses on a particular problem or issue. For example, it might examine a service, such as in-flight food, or it might address how British Airways is faring on a specific route, or it might evaluate the effectiveness of a particular ad campaign.

The unit's overarching mission is to act as a surrogate for customers in assessing the airline's performance. "That means using criteria that customers apply in judging how we're doing rather than those a manager might use to judge how he or she is doing," says Christopher A. Swan, the unit's head. "They're often quite different. Managers, quite naturally, tend to look at their operation's performance through rose-tinted glasses."

Take reservation agents' response time. The marketplace performance unit measures the entire time it takes for a customer to get through to an agent, including the time the phone is ringing and the time the customer is on hold until he or she is transferred to an available agent. "In addition, we measure how many people going through the process get so hacked off they hang up," Swan says. In contrast, airlines with a management perspective might measure only how many times the phone rings before the system answers it.

Waiting lines at check-in desks furnish another example. An airline with a management perspective might measure the number of minutes it took for customers to get to the front of the line. But when the marketplace performance unit asked customers, it found they were more concerned with the length of the lines and the rate at which they moved.

The marketplace performance unit also provides a critical means of measuring improvement in customer service. The unit's first assignment was to have staffers travel on British Airways' flights and submit regular reports on exactly what was done at what time during the flights. Soon after, it began benchmarking British Airways against competitors' flights.

"We look at everything down to when and whether the flight attendants served the packets of peanuts," Swan says. "It may seem small, but each customer comes away with an extremely personalized view of how a company served him. If a customer happens to be a peanut buff, the worst thing that can happen on a short domestic flight is for that person not to be offered a packet of peanuts. He'll remember that we didn't give him a packet while our competitors did."

This attention to detail led British Airways to overhaul the food service on its flights between Britain and Japan. The airline had prided itself on providing proper Japanese food, but when the marketplace performance unit investigated how Japanese customers perceived the food, the polite response was, "For Westerners, you're doing quite well." It turned out that details that British Airways had not realized were important–such as the shape and color of the dishes holding the food and how they were arranged on the tray–mattered significantly to Japanese customers. The unit also learned that the Japanese prefer to eat small amounts of food relatively frequently and that what they really love in the middle of the night are pot noodles, a kind of noodle stew.

The top 20 executives of British Airways can call on the marketplace performance unit to help explore issues, but the unit also can take the initiative when a competitor introduces a new service or when the unit's data or data collected by the customer relations department suggest that a problem or threat exists. When the unit has identified a problem, it presents its findings to senior managers, who then debate the possible solutions and create a plan of action. "The unit is not just a mystery shopper or a market-research department that produces numbers and then is ignored. It has the ear of the entire top management as an honest broker of customer information," says Marshall, whom the unit's members call "our champion."

In many instances, the marketplace performance unit's customer perspective has caused British Airways to take the less obvious path. For example, when a competitor began offering free limousine service to business-class and first-class customers arriving on long-haul flights, management asked the unit to determine whether British Airways should follow suit. It discovered that British Airways' customers were ambivalent about such a service. What they really wanted on arrival after a long night flight, they said, was a place to freshen up and relax until it was time to leave for their business appointments. This discovery led British Airways to establish airport facilities to which overnight passengers arriving in Britain on intercontinental flights could go. "It's important to test whether something is what customers really want or is just what management thinks they want," Swan says. "Our unit is not supposed to fit comfortably with the rest of the organization. We're supposed to generate creative conflict. We're another reality check."

**Originally published in November–December 1995**
**Reprint 95607**

# Surviving Success

## *An Interview with the Nature Conservancy's John Sawhill*

ALICE HOWARD AND
JOAN MAGRETTA

### Executive Summary

CAN AN ORGANIZATION WITH a four-decade track record of growth avoid becoming the victim of its own success? Since the Nature Conservancy was founded in 1951, it has worked to save threatened habitats and species by buying and setting aside land. Year by year, the number of acres under its protection has increased, membership has risen, and donations have grown.

The leader of any nonprofit company might justifiably envy the Conservancy's performance, but its president and CEO, John Sawhill, isn't satisfied. Since taking the job in 1990, Sawhill has led a major shift in strategy with far-reaching implications for the day-to-day activities of the organization's 2,000 employees. He believes that the Conservancy must change now to achieve its mission over the long term.

In this interview, he discusses the challenges inherent in refocusing a large, successful, mission-driven organization. Chief among them has been the need to integrate economic growth with environmental protection. The Conservancy has therefore promoted development projects that are compatible with the preservation of species and habitats. And to chart the progress of these and other projects, Sawhill has moved the organization beyond strategic plans that express only good intention; instead, the Conservancy has devised concrete performance measures that allow it to convert its mission statement into specific goals.

John Sawhill's career has spanned the social, public, and private sectors. He was president of New York University from 1975 to 1979, deputy secretary of the Department of Energy during the Carter administration, and a director at McKinsey & Company from 1981 to 1990.

---

*Can an organization with a four-decade track record of growth avoid becoming the victim of its own success? Since the Nature Conservancy was founded in 1951, it has worked to save threatened habitats and species by buying and setting aside land. Year by year, the number of acres under its protection has increased, membership has risen, and donations have grown.*

*Today the Conservancy manages some 1,600 separate preserves—the largest private system of nature sanctuaries in the world—from more than 200 offices spread from Maine to Micronesia. With an estimated $1 billion in assets, it has become one of the largest conservation organizations in the world. Among its peers, the Conser-*

*vancy has had the fastest growth rate during the 1990s. (See the exhibit "The Nature Conservancy at a Glance.")*

*The leader of any nonprofit company might justifiably envy the Conservancy's performance, but its president and CEO, John Sawhill, isn't satisfied. Since taking the job in 1990, the 59-year-old Sawhill has led a major shift in strategy with far-reaching implications for the day-to-day activities of the organization's 2,000 employees. He believes that the Conservancy must change now to achieve its mission over the long term—and that the organization's mission holds the key to guiding that change.*

*Sawhill's career has spanned the social, public, and private sectors. He was president of New York University from 1975 to 1979, deputy secretary of the Department of Energy during the Carter administration, and a director at McKinsey & Company from 1981 to 1990.*

*In this interview with HBR editors Alice Howard and Joan Magretta, Sawhill discusses the challenges inherent in refocusing a large, successful, mission-driven organization.*

---

***In 1990, Peter Drucker referred to the Nature Conservancy as "the best example of a winning strategy in a nonprofit institution." Yet you are leading the organization through significant change. Was Drucker wrong?***

Sometimes an organization is slow to accept change because it's doing so well. Peter Drucker was a teacher of mine, and one of the things he said to me was that the worst thing that could happen to any organization is 40 years of unbroken success.

The Conservancy has always had a very clear mission: to preserve plants and animals and special habitats that represent the diversity of life. We are completely focused on that mission; it drives everything we do. We had to change, though, because while we were doing a lot of good conservation work, there were more and more signs that we were not making significant progress toward accomplishing our mission.

---

### *The Nature Conservancy at a Glance*

**Total acres protected since 1955**

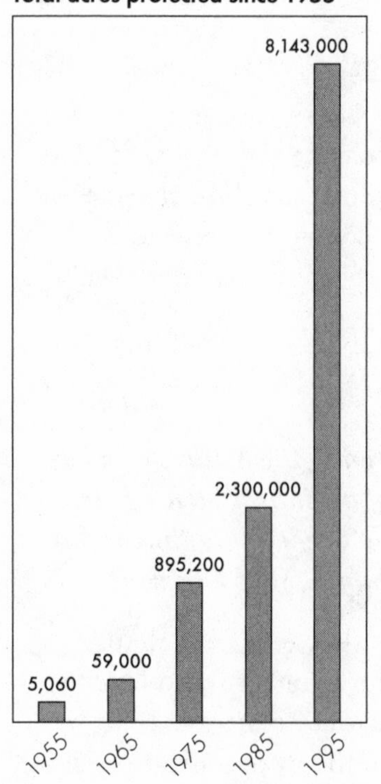


**Total membership**

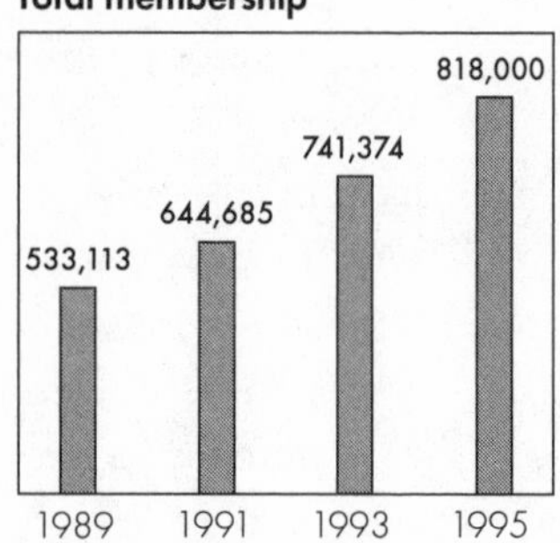


**Annual operating budget**
(in thousands)

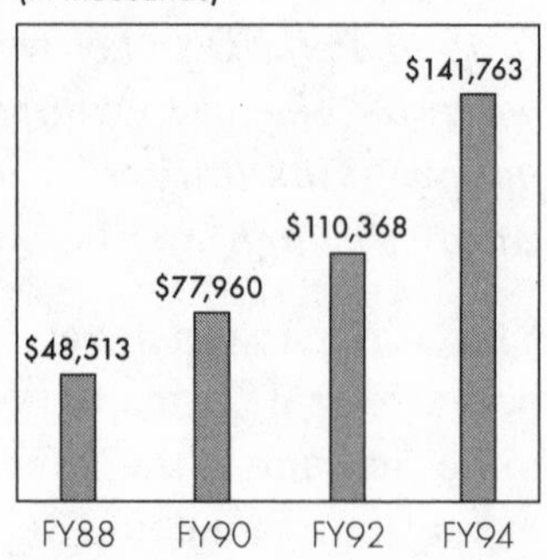

### *Your mission wasn't conservation?*

Our mission hasn't changed; our approach has. You might call our original approach a Noah's Ark strategy. For four decades, the Conservancy focused almost exclusively on setting aside critical habitats for endangered species. In practice, that meant buying the specific piece of wetlands, forest, or prairie that supported a particular species or natural community. Like Noah, the Conservancy was intent on building an ark—or, more accurately, building a lot of little arks.

That approach was easily measurable. In the past, whenever we wanted to know how we were doing, we could simply count the acres we'd protected and check our membership figures. By those traditional measures of success, we were doing just fine. But we started to realize that those measures weren't giving us the right information. We had a terrific collection of preserves, but there was growing concern about the lasting effectiveness of our conservation strategy. The more we looked at the scientific data, the more we became concerned that our arks were springing leaks. In other words, places we thought were protected really weren't. That wasn't a sudden revelation. People in the field were talking about it, but nobody knew whether it was true or false or what we should do about it.

### *How did you come to believe that you might have a problem?*

Our experience with Schenob Brook in Massachusetts, for example, helped to alert us. A number of years after we had acquired that property, we were alarmed to find that the bog turtle population was declining. It turned out that activities outside our preserve were affecting the water that the turtles ultimately depended on. Here was the problem: We thought we could buy a piece of land, fence it off, and thereby protect whatever was in that preserve. But that thinking proved mistaken, which meant that our old performance measures—such as how much land we had acquired for conservation—weren't valid indicators of institutional progress.

We simply couldn't go on with business-as-usual. For-profit companies can look at their financial statements every day to see how they're doing: They're either making money or not. Without the discipline of the bottom line, it's easier for nonprofit organizations to get off track. For the Conservancy, science is really our bottom line.

And science led us to our new strategy. It became clear that we needed to influence land use in larger areas surrounding the kinds of core preserves that we had traditionally acquired. Now we focus on much larger landscapes, areas we call Last Great Places. That way we can work to ensure that the economic and recreational activities going on outside the preserves don't undermine the balance of life inside them.

***How did you arrive at this new approach?***

When I joined the Conservancy in 1990, the first thing I did was to initiate a review of our strategy. Like most other environmental organizations, we had grown rapidly in the 1980s. Some of the basic systems we were using to run the enterprise hadn't kept up with that growth: Our financial system was not producing reports on time, our marketing system was not giving us accurate, up-to-date information on our members, and our personnel systems were antiquated. In addition, the board of governors was concerned that the organization was becoming fragmented. It needed leadership, it needed to be pulled together, it needed to have a clear vision of where it was going. But it was our strategic planning process itself that brought the fundamental need for a new strategy to the surface.

*Can you describe that process?*

I asked our senior managers to identify the most capable of the up-and-coming managers in the organization—its future leaders—and I picked four of them for the strategy task force. Those four are still with the organization, and they're all in leadership roles today. I tried to have some balance in expertise and in geography: We had two scientists, one fundraiser, and one person who was involved in land acquisition; they came from Florida, Hawaii, North Carolina, and from our international program. The head of the group was someone I'd recruited from outside who brought planning expertise but lacked conservation experience. For four months, these people left their jobs and came together to work on the strategic plan.

***"We're concentrating more on strategies that address what I consider to be* the *conservation issue of the 1990s: integrating economic growth with environmental protection."***

I spent about 25% of my time on this effort, meeting frequently with the planning team and with the different groups that make up the Nature Conservancy: our state directors, chapter trustees, and national board. We conducted a series of meetings and informational sessions around the country for volunteers and staff. That was important. When you rely on people's love for the organization's mission, rather than on their career ambitions or financial incentives, it is absolutely critical to have a highly participative decision-making process. Many companies limit real participation in strategic decision making to senior managers. Their top-level managers get the most powerful people in the company together, convince them of something, and then assume that everyone else will follow. The best companies, in contrast, make an effort to get more people involved.

Our task force conducted about 75 interviews all over the organization, which helped bring to the surface many of the ideas and concerns that had been floating around. It also interviewed outsiders, including scientists and people in other conservation organizations. After five months of discussion, the organization coalesced around the new strategy of larger landscapes as well as a variety of new challenges. We were going to have to build our science capability and develop new, riskier conservation strategies.

***What was risky about your new conservation strategies?***

We're concentrating more on strategies that address what I consider to be *the* conservation issue of the 1990s: integrating economic growth with environmental protection. How do you protect a species when the chief threat to that species comes from 100 miles away? We have to broaden our scope.

The risk comes from our getting deeply involved in places where people live and work, because people are as much a part of the landscape as the plants and animals we're trying to protect. So we have to find ways to work with communities and businesses as partners, and that won't happen if conservation means throwing people out of work or driving companies out of business. Promoting compatible economic development has therefore become a strategic imperative for us.

***What do you mean by compatible development?***

It means that when we're trying to do a project to protect a landscape or one of our Last Great Places, we have to be concerned with both economic and environmental issues. We have to be sure that there are jobs for people, even as we are trying to protect natural areas. This dual concern has gotten us involved in a number of economic ventures that may seem a bit removed from traditional land conservation measures.

The Virginia Coast Reserve is probably our most ambitious undertaking in this area. That project began in 1969 in traditional Conservancy fashion. We bought a chain of barrier islands on Virginia's eastern shore—about 40,000 acres in all—to protect both migratory birds and shorebirds as well as the islands' natural communities. But by the mid-1980s, we realized that the islands were part of a much larger ecological system. The birds on the islands were dependent on the health of the coastal waters, and the waters were dependent on how land was used on the mainland. All of a sudden, we were looking at much larger and more complex conservation initiatives.

Science drove our new approach. We knew that the birds depended on salt marshes and mudflats behind the islands, but we were not sure how to protect those marine resources. You see, the Conservancy had never worked on the water. We bought the *land.* You can't buy water, except for maybe an inland lake and Western water rights; navigable waters are all part of the public domain. At the same time, the waters around those islands were the heart of the ecological system. How were we going to protect the salt marshes and mudflats? We just stared at the blackboard until eventually we realized, to put it simply, that water runs downhill. In short, what happens on the mainland is what governs the health of the water surrounding it.

So we started to address mainland uses of the watershed. We put together a team—they were called Four Scientists and an M.B.A.—to develop a strategic plan and think through how we would go about conserving this area. We spent more than a year identifying and analyzing the activities that pose the greatest threats to the whole system. We concluded that permanent residential and resort development on the mainland was far worse for the watershed than the traditional use of the land, which was farming. If you have too many septic systems, wastewater overloads the coastal waters with nutrients, which in turn produce too much algae, which kills the marine life. Once those relationships became clear, we had our answer. We had to find a way to encourage and promote low-density development on the waterfront.

In typical Conservancy fashion, our first move was to buy more land. We started acquiring key mainland properties on the seaside waterfront—not to manage them as nature preserves but rather to resell them with permanent restrictions prohibiting environmentally incompatible uses. As a result, we succeeded in keeping more of the land maintained for farming. We also felt that unless we could do something about the area's weak economy, there would be too much pressure for development in ways inconsistent with our conservation objectives. And so we're trying to find new, low-impact businesses to come into the area, profit from the eastern shore's comparative advantages, and provide jobs for people.

***If your core capabilities as an organization are in science and real estate, what you're describing sounds like a real departure. Do you have to go outside the organization for people?***

Yes, for two new skills. First, we need community-development organizing skills. We typically hire someone who will live in the area, be rooted in the community, and will work with other local people to build and strengthen a conservation ethic. Second, we need business-development and marketing skills. For the Virginia project, we recruited the former vice president and chief business officer of Colonial Williamsburg to help manage a new for-profit company called the Virginia Eastern Shore Sustainable Development Corporation, which has three goals: profitability, job creation, and environmental protection. We felt that the enterprise had to be for-profit in order to succeed. On the other hand, we and our investors realized that we couldn't expect to make venture capital returns.

The trick to economic development anywhere is to identify what is special about the place—its comparative advantages—and to build on that. Also, there is strength in diversity, so our strategy is not to look for 2 different 50% solutions but 50 different 2% solutions. Specifically, our goal with the Virginia shore project is to create 50 small businesses that will generate 250 jobs over the next five years. The company will initially focus on developing and marketing nature-tourism programs and related services, which are a natural fit given the region's beauty and proximity to major population centers. In addition, it will try to take advantage of the area's strong agricultural base to develop and market high-quality, high-margin specialty foods and organic produce. Today the farmers are growing commodity crops and losing money.

***"If a species is nearing extinction, we've let things go too far."***

If we're as successful as we hope to be, the project will become a model we'll use elsewhere. We're very excited about this venture—the spark is lit.

Our mission leads us to this kind of activity because once you say you're going to work on the scale of an entire landscape to protect biological resources, you've touched the tar baby whether you like it or not. You're in the community-development business and the conservation business; the two are inextricably linked.

***As you learn more about sustainable development, do you find areas where a species' survival and economic activity clash irreconcilably? What about the battle in the Pacific Northwest between environmentalists and the logging industry over the spotted owl?***

Obviously, there are no easy answers to conflicts like those, but such clashes are not inevitable. The controversies surrounding the Endangered Species Act show that people on all sides are not doing a good job in planning and prevention. The lesson to be learned is this: The best way to avoid divisive conflicts over endangered species is to get out in front of the issue, to address the problem before it becomes a crisis. It's just plain bad policy to wait until a plant or animal is on the brink of extinction before taking action. Too often, we wait until we have to send in the cavalry when a little diplomacy beforehand could have avoided the whole mess.

If we get to the point where a species is nearing extinction, we've let things go too far. Whether it's an owl or a gnatcatcher or a salmon—these creatures are not responsible for the decline of industries. Their near extinction is usually symptomatic of a larger problem. The plight of the spotted owl in the Pacific Northwest, for instance, suggests that a once-plentiful resource, the old-growth forest, is in trouble. And we depend on that resource for future, sustainable economic development.

On my desk, I have a little sign that says, "If you're not the lead dog, the view never changes." Businesses and communities that get out in front on environmental issues will have an enormous competitive advantage over those that stall, file lawsuits, or simply bury their heads in the sand.

### *How are business leaders doing on environmental issues today?*

Some of the most innovative and competitive companies I know have been in the forefront of energy conservation and the search for less-polluting methods of operation. Perhaps the bigger problem is the perception that environmental protection and economic vitality are at odds with each other. An unfortunate legacy of the 1980s seems to be that many in the business community still perceive *environmentalism* as a dirty word. At the same time, many environmentalists seem to have nothing good to say about the corporate world.

You might call the result of these hostile perceptions the "spotted owl syndrome": a kind of economic-environmental gridlock. The symptoms are easy enough to detect. Endless litigation. Stubborn, entrenched interests. All-or-nothing thinking and either-or choices. And on the sidelines, lots of lawyers cheering the combatants on.

***How do your new strategies break the gridlock?***

We try to help companies find a constructive approach to what they want to do. If an oil company wants to drill in an environmentally sensitive area, we won't say, Don't drill. Instead we ask, Is there any way you can drill and not harm the area's ecological integrity? Let's try to develop a drilling plan that won't disturb the wildlife habitat. We believe in partnerships. Consequently, we seek to work with a broad variety of people and organizations: individuals, businesses, government, other nonprofits, universities, you name it. We'll work with anyone—from gigantic multinational companies to an individual farmer or fisherman—who will help us achieve our mission.

In recent years, for example, we've become quite active in mitigation; that is, in helping to find solutions that offset environmental damage. In 1992, the Walt Disney Company wanted to expand its operations in Orlando, Florida, to build its wild animal theme park. The state, however, was concerned about damage to wetlands. A solution was jointly engineered by Disney, the Nature Conservancy, and local, state, and federal agencies: In exchange for permission to develop the Orlando site, which will affect about 340 acres of wetlands over a 20-year period, Disney agreed to purchase, protect, and restore 8,500 acres of wetlands and wilderness in central Florida. Disney will donate this land in phases to the Conservancy and provide an endowment to make sure that we can continue to operate it. By the way, these kinds of mitigation agreements will become more and more popular in the future. They offer creative, nonregulatory solutions that help the environment without hurting the ability of businesses to develop their valuable assets.

Another way we help break the gridlock is by using our expertise to help companies with site planning and land management. Information from our species inventory can be invaluable in helping planners site power lines, pipelines, construction projects, or roads. A little biological homework before-hand can avert costly delays, lawsuits, and negative public opinion.

A recent example is instructive. The Georgia-Pacific Corporation wanted to consider how it might contribute to conservation but not give up all its rights to harvest timber in perpetuity on a particular piece of property. The company called in the Nature Conservancy and said, "Let's think about this together. Which parts of this area should be permanently set aside, and which might be selectively logged or logged at some future time using our normal methods?" We talked about it and ultimately signed a contract that gives the two organizations equal rights in determining future timber harvests on the property. The Conservancy and Georgia-Pacific each have one vote, and questions of future harvests must be resolved unanimously. Instead of getting into a situation where it might have incurred opposition from environmental groups, Georgia-Pacific worked out a plan that they found very satisfactory, and it also got a lot of good publicity for having taken that approach.

***What major challenges do you face as you work more in various partnership arrangements?***

We have a strong results-oriented culture. One former

director of the U.S. Fish and Wildlife Service described the Conservancy as "all action and no talk." We like to get things done and, as we all know, the best way to get things done is to do it yourself. What we have to realize is that in a partnership it's *not* our job to get things done on our own. Our job is to help our partners by giving them the tools they need.

One of the fundamental challenges that every manager faces—how to measure success—has become even more difficult for us because of the complex objectives of our partnerships. (See "From Good Intentions to Good Performance" at the end of this article.) As I said earlier, it was a lot easier when we measured our success by the number of acres we bought or the number of dollars we raised. But the compatible development initiatives that are critical to our mission don't fit neatly into those categories, and it may take years to tell how effective our projects have been.

At the same time, an organization has to set goals and objectives annually to make sure that people understand clearly what is expected of them. One of the problems common in nonprofits is that people don't have specific, measurable goals and objectives. So, for instance, we'll set fund-raising goals for a program such as the Oklahoma Tallgrass Prairie Preserve, in which our aim was to raise the $15 million we needed to buy the land. With a project such as the Virginia shore, the goals might include the number of jobs to be created.

Some of the objectives critical to our mission are difficult to quantify, but we can still use them as goals. For instance, if we are to succeed, we have to establish programs that can serve as models for future conservation work. Our state program in Hawaii set a standard in rain forest protection, but we measured its success not just by what we accomplished in Hawaii but also by our ability to apply what we learned there about island ecology to other areas in the Pacific. Today we are successfully extending the Hawaiian model to Indonesia, Papua New Guinea, and Micronesia. We're always trying to build on our strengths. In that way, the "transportability" of programs is an important measure of success for us.

***You alluded earlier to changes in your science organization. What changes did you make?***

We set priorities for conservation—our operating strategy, in a sense—based on objective, scientific data about species and habitats. Although we appreciate the value of beautiful landscapes as much as anyone else, we won't try to save a place unless it harbors a rare species or an important habitat. To put it another way, we have always been in the science business, not the pretty business.

But even though we have always thought of ourselves as a science-driven organization, we have long needed to integrate science more effectively into our conservation planning. After undertaking the strategic review, we discovered that we were actually in two separate businesses. On the one hand, we maintain the world's best databases on species and their habitats, and our science business provided information on threatened areas both for the Conservancy and for outsiders such as government agencies and corporations. On the other hand, we were in the business of buying land and protecting it. It wasn't always clear that we were successfully integrating our scientific information with our conservation work. We had to use science to understand better the ecological processes at work on the land that interested us.

We also needed new capabilities in the area of stewardship; that is, in managing properties once we acquire them. To bring about that major change, we hired specialists in such fields as fire ecology, weed control, and biohydrology—a subspecialty of water management. People with skills in those areas help us understand how to manage properties to best protect their native plants and animals.

***Were there any changes in your donor strategy as a result of the strategic review?***

I wouldn't say that our strategy has changed, but we did learn some things that have helped keep us on course. We have always had a clear donor strategy that fit our mission. Some people at the Conservancy think our customers are the plants and animals we're trying to save, but our real customers are the donors who buy our product, and that product is protected landscapes. Because fund-raising takes place locally, we have organized around local chapters in every state. Our target market is the broad and growing segment of people who love the outdoors and want to preserve it—and who are looking for groups that are achieving tangible results. They like the fact that we use private-sector techniques to achieve our objectives, that we protect the environment the old-fashioned way: We buy it.

***"We think of ourselves as Adam Smith with a green thumb."***

We have made a conscious, strategic decision to rely on individual donors and not to become too heavily dependent on government, because we want to be clearly identified as a private organization, one that is financed privately and uses free-market techniques. We think of ourselves as Adam Smith with a green thumb.

Our nonconfrontational strategy gives us a very broad and stable base of support that runs the whole political spectrum—George Bush and Bill Clinton are both financial supporters—and you know, we like it that way. I would guess that the only thing all our members could agree on is the importance of the work we do.

In the strategic review, we identified two fundamental strengths that we never want to tamper with. First, our success in fund-raising really stems from the decentralized nature of our organization. Every single one of our operating units has fund-raising responsibility. We have a culture that says if you want to do something, then you have to go out and find the money for it. You can't turn to the development department and say, "Gee, I'd really like to do this great thing—you guys go find the money for me." Being decentralized is also important because people give to people they know. Donors want to get to know members of their community, to build relationships with them, to help them understand what the organization is really about. That's the most powerful fund-raising tool we have.

Second, our market research has shown that people appreciate the Conservancy's positive message. Much environmental activism is based on bad news, which spurs people to action by forcing them to confront unpleasant realities. Our strategy lets us tell people good news. We buy a place or we take some other action that yields positive results. No matter how our strategy changes, those two aspects of our work are the bedrock on which we build.

We're asked to deviate from our mission all the time. Donors say they'll give us more money if we get involved in, for example, population. A few years ago, one of the big foundations offered us several hundred thousand dollars to start a program on population. But that's not what we're good at; it's not an area in which we have expertise. So we said no.

Whenever someone comes to me with a proposal for an exciting new Nature Conservancy project, I ask myself the same question: Given our limited resources and the enormous challenges we face, how will this advance our mission of protecting biodiversity? We often have to say no to projects that, however tantalizing, are tangential to our goals.

***Have any organizational changes flowed from the new strategy?***

Yes. For years we had the kind of management committee you'd find in almost every organization: a war council composed of the heads of the major units. Its members spent all their time talking about day-to-day operations, and conservation strategy was relegated to the secondary spot. I became dissatisfied with that way of operating; it just didn't give us the right focus on our mission. It is a common problem in organizations that the mundane triumphs over the strategic.

One of the amazing consequences of our strategy shift was that about a year ago the management group voted to disband itself. We were searching for a way to focus on the most advanced thinking in conservation, a way to propel the organization forward on conservation issues. In place of the old structure, we have established a conservation committee, which discusses and debates issues affecting our mission, and an operations committee, which handles administrative issues. We've also made significant changes in the faces around the table. Instead of the old war council, the traditional horizontal slice at the top, we took a vertical slice of the organization for both groups. We now have a mixture of people from throughout the organization, including practitioners from the field, people with dirt under their fingernails. Finally, we created a third entity, a management council, comprising roughly 150 managers from all parts of the organization. That group will meet once a year to review the work done by the conservation and operations committees.

The new structure replaces a tighter management team that had consisted only of senior staff, and it represents a real shift in management philosophy. The early returns are positive. We have been able to hone further our conservation agenda and eliminate layers of bureaucratic review for day-to-day decision making.

Our new conservation strategy demands a high level of creativity from people throughout the organization, and any organization that has grown as we have must guard against bureaucratic tendencies. I don't think you can get people to be more entrepreneurial unless you make them responsible for a piece of the organization and give them control of their own destinies. We can give people in the field a lot of autonomy as long as we have absolute clarity about our mission and our core values.

Usually when we have a successful program it's because the person running it is entrepreneurial and knows how to take advantage of opportunities, mobilize resources, and attract a good board. The success of any program often comes down to the skills, energy, and leadership of the individual heading it. The difference in results between two programs is generally not that we did it one way here and one way there, and that the first way was much better than the second. Usually the difference is that in one case an individual figured out what the community's needs were and developed a program that met those needs.

In our organization, the state director is usually the prime mover. The team obviously plays an important role, but if you don't have a strong leader, it's hard for the team to operate effectively. So we spend a lot of time and care recruiting our state directors. I personally interview all of them before they're hired. What I most want to know about them is how entrepreneurial they are, how creative they are, what new things they're doing.

***Has there been much resistance within your organization to the changes you've set in motion?***

People in this organization are deeply committed to its mission. They care about it; they think about it all the time. Fundamentally, it's what drives them. There is something about a nonprofit's mission that motivates people by closely aligning personal values with professional values. Maybe there's a lesson here for corporations. When mission comes first, people are more open to change: They accept changes that would probably cause a lot of anxiety if they weren't committed to the larger purpose. We invested an enormous amount of time and energy in the strategy process, and once we got it done, our people generally accepted the changes. They were convinced that the new strategy was the right way to achieve our mission.

***What is the most satisfying part of your job?***

I tell people I have the best job in America. First, I work with committed, energetic, bright people. Second, I do something that I regard as extremely important. Protecting natural areas and leaving them for future generations is one of the most important things we could possibly do;

it's leaving the world a better place than it would otherwise be. So I'm motivated by the significance of the task. A lot of businesspeople think that someday they'll do a stint in government to make their contribution to society. They ought to think about working in a nonprofit instead. Not only will they get a lot more done, but nonprofit work is also much more rewarding than government service. I can say that because I've done both.

---

## From Good Intentions to Good Performance

***by John Sawhill***

PERFORMANCE MEASURES ARE the vehicle for converting a mission statement into specific goals. One of the things I found when I first looked at the Conservancy's plans was that they never defined success. The plans detailed a whole series of activities that we were going to conduct, but they never suggested how we would know when we had achieved our goals. Today we require a clear definition of success for every Last Great Place project we undertake. We developed a planning format that defined the *system* we were trying to protect, the *stresses* to that ecological system, the *source* of the stresses, the *strategy* for dealing with those stresses, and how we would measure our *success*.

This plan became known as the 5-S format, but it was just a way of communicating to the organization what a good protection plan would contain. Take our Fish Creek Project in northeastern Indiana; we're trying to protect a system of freshwater mussels there. The stress comes from excessive silt in the water, and the sources of the silt are two agricultural practices: tillage up to the water's edge and fall plowing. Farmers can't practice no-till agriculture without expensive special equipment. Our strategy is to lower that barrier by subsidizing 15% of the equipment's cost if a farmer agrees to practice no-till agriculture on a minimum of 250 acres for at least three years. We have three key measures of success: the number of acres under the no-till method, the silt levels in the water, and the size of the mussel population in Fish Creek.

In contrast, earlier strategic plans had been created more for fund-raising purposes than for setting a clear direction for the organization. I knew we needed concrete goals, objectives, and action plans. The old plans were full of good intentions, not performance measures. They were characterized by phrases like "We need to work more effectively with the local community" or "We should try to influence public land managers to do a better job."

Ultimately, we have to measure our success by the species we save. But in the short term, to find out if we're on the right track, we have to learn what we should be monitoring. As we build our scientific capabilities in the area of stewardship, we learn what measures to take and how to take them. Are the ecosystems we're trying to protect maintaining their functions, for example, in purifying water and maintaining soil? We're trying to develop measures that can answer such questions.

**Originally published in September–October 1995**
**Reprint 95508**

# Governing the Family-Owned Enterprise

## *An Interview with Finland's Krister Ahlström*

JOAN MAGRETTA


### Executive Summary

WHEN KRISTER AHLSTRÖM BECAME the CEO of one of Europe's preeminent family-owned companies in 1982, he saw immediately that the company would not survive in an era of global competition without a complete overhaul of its strategy. His first task: to shed weak businesses and focus the company on a few core areas where it would have to build new capabilities.

But Ahlström quickly learned that he could not change the company's strategic direction without tackling the most basic issues of corporate governance. In this interview, he describes the process that led the Ahlström family to a new understanding of its relationship to the company. Although governance has become a controversial topic in publicly owned companies, it has always been a far more contentious issue–if a less visible one–in private companies. In family businesses, the complex mix of emotions and business needs makes governance questions particularly difficult to answer. For example, how should the family, the board, and the business interact? And who should determine the direction of the company? In the Ahlstrom Corporation's case, the family arrived at a definition of its role as enlightened–not passive–owners. And it developed several governance and communication mechanisms to support that role: a Family Council, a Family Assembly, formal training for the family's next generation, and a written document of values and policies that functions like a constitution.

---

*Is a company's primary responsibility to its shareholders or its stakeholders? What is the proper role of a company's board, and who should serve on it? To whom and for what are managers accountable?*

*In the last ten years, a series of shock waves in the once staid realm of corporate governance has ignited a reexamination of these most basic of governance questions. Increasingly, we see signs that the old equilibrium is giving way. Large institutional investors are no longer content to be passive owners. At the same time, boards are stepping up–sometimes under pressure–to claim a more activist role.*

*While the debate has erupted with new urgency and high visibility in publicly owned corporations, governance has always been a contentious–although usually private–issue in family-owned enterprises. And in most of the world, family-owned enterprises dominate the business landscape. Even in the United States, family ownership is more prevalent than most people realize. It is estimated that over a third of the Fortune 500 are family owned or dominated; for the world economy as a whole, the number is certainly over 50%.*

*As CEO of his family's $3 billion holding company, Krister Ahlström has been grappling with governance issues for more than a decade. The Ahlstrom Corporation was founded by Antti Ahlström in 1851 and is wholly owned by his roughly 200 descendants. (See "Ahlstrom's Roots" at the end of this article.) Today few family members actually work in the company, but the family controls the board. Krister Ahlström will retire in the winter of 1998 after leading the company through a 15-year transformation.*

*Ahlström joined the family business in 1982 after a successful career at Wärtsilä, a large Finnish conglomerate. He saw immediately that without a complete overhaul of its business strategy, the company would not survive in an era of global competition. His first task: to shed weak businesses and focus the company on a few core areas where it would have to build the capabilities to compete effectively in world markets.*

*But he quickly learned that he could not change the company's strategic direction without also leading the Ahlström family to a new understanding of its relationship to the company. In this interview with HBR editor-at-large Joan Magretta, Krister Ahlström describes the changes that now allow the family to interact with the company as enlightened—not passive—owners. The transformation, as Ahlström describes it, began with "a big fight" that almost led to his ouster as CEO.*

---

***Until you became CEO in 1982, your entire career had taken place outside the family business. What did you find when you arrived?***

Back then, Ahlstrom was an $800 million company. Effectively, all our operations were located in Finland. (See the chart "Ahlstrom: 15 Years of Change.") In the decades following World War I, Finland's economy was closed to foreign competition. In a protected economy, local companies tend to expand into other domestic businesses. Look at companies in India today and you see the same thing. So Ahlstrom went through a period of diversification from the forest industry, accumulating a portfolio consisting of almost 60 different businesses. We went into glass products, including even art glass. And we were in building materials, in machinery, and you name it. By 1982, however, most of our businesses were not in good shape either operationally or strategically.

---

### Ahlstrom: 15 Years of Change

*In 1981, Ahlstrom was an $800 million company focused on the forest industry and based in Finland. By 1996, it was a $3.3 billion technology-based diversified multinational with a global reach. The chart below shows how the company has grown and changed its geographic focus.*

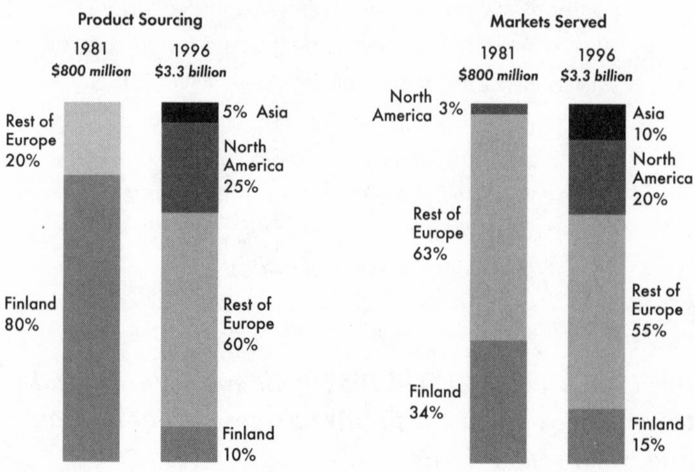

Every new CEO has to form his own view of the company he is going to lead. An insider is apt to ask, Are we doing things right? Because I came from outside the company, it was easier for me to ask, Are we doing the right things?

*And were you?*

I'm afraid not. We asked one consulting firm to assess our situation. They came to us with such a pessimistic view that we asked another firm for a second opinion. Their assessment was even more pessimistic. Out of 60 businesses, about 40 were just mediocre. We had some tough calls to make about which to keep. Only 3 of our businesses seemed really promising. And 15 were in such bad shape that not only did we have to sell, we were advised to do so quickly.

*Did you follow that advice?*

That's where the story gets interesting. The largest business in trouble was bulk paper. But our mill was synonymous with the Ahlstrom name. Despite our diversification, everyone knew us as a forest industry company. The mill actually accounted for only 20% of our revenues, but most people thought the number was much higher.

The mill was losing money. The forest industry was consolidating, and fixing the problem would have required major capital infusions. It usually doesn't make sense for a family-owned company to be in such a capital-intensive industry, because to get the money you need for the business you inevitably have to give some control to outside investors. We didn't want to do that.

So I went to the board and said we had to sell the business. Remember that in Scandinavia we have a two-tier system in which management reports to the board. There is a clear separation between the deciding power of the board and the executing role of management. And so I needed the board's approval to sell the mill.

Not only did I not get their approval, but the members were too upset at the time to listen to the facts. The board was dominated then by third-generation thinking. It consisted of family members along with some long-time friends and former executives of the company. I was in my forties, and I belong to the fourth generation of the family. I was very harshly criticized.

***Why such a strong reaction?***

The mill had such symbolic value in Finland that many family members were shocked. They thought I was ripping the heart out of the company. Such strong reactions are not unusual in family companies. Their boards often get emotionally involved in management decisions. They care deeply, but they may not always be on top of the business realities. So when you try to make changes, you often run into strongly held beliefs. The attitude was, "We have always done it this way. We have always been in that business. Our tradition is built on our presence in such and such a place."

***"I realized there was a huge gap between the perception of the owners and the business realities."***

I persisted. A year later, as the mill continued to lose money, it became harder to ignore the facts. In 1986, we pushed ahead and found a buyer, but the decision to sell was only narrowly carried in the board. The problem was not only with the board. Many of the other owners—the

200 family members—did not really understand or accept the need for change.

*Has their view changed?*

Yes. Looking back, we all see this sale as a watershed. From a purely business standpoint, we had to divest our heaviest cash drain before we could start to build our future. More important, selling the mill marked the beginning of a long process that enabled the Ahlström family to jump over its own shadow, so to speak, and to change its relationship with the company. The battle over the divestiture taught me a lesson. I realized that we could not go on as a company as long as there was a huge gap between the perceptions of the owners and the business realities. We had to do something to address that problem, both with the board and the family.

*What did you do?*

First, I reached into my own experience. In the early 1970s, there was a strongly adversarial relationship between management and labor unions in Finland, and I had worked in a particularly hostile situation at another large Finnish company. If you want to learn negotiation skills, a labor-management struggle is the right situation for it.

I realized that the same methods that had been effective with the labor unions could help me reach the family and the board with my messages. In dealing with a union, you must get past the stubborn people and directly influence opinion at the floor level. You must encourage workers with the right disposition to come forward and become active as leaders. I applied those lessons to Ahlstrom. I was helped by some members of the younger generation. It took 20 years to change Finland's labor unions, and it took almost as long with the Ahlström family. In both cases, a big part of the problem was a lack of information.

*What else did you do?*

I turned to the management literature for help. And what a revelation that was! I found miles of shelves with books on management. They all concerned strategy, how to compete in the marketplace, how to organize a company for maximum effectiveness. But there was hardly any literature on how to govern companies. And nothing on how to govern family companies.

It was as if all the management experts overlooked the simple fact that every company has owners and a board, and that there are all kinds of pressures on top of the strategic and operating issues. Frankly, I was surprised. I happen to be interested in history, and most of history is about governance. It's not about the nitty-gritty of running a country; it's about how the country is governed.

*What does governance mean for a company?*

It means how a company's values are created and upheld, how you decide what course the company should take. It's not enough to say you're going to make a profit. You must also say, in broad terms, *how* you're going to do that. In particular industries or in any industry at all? With active or passive owners? Using ethical methods or cutting corners? There was very little in the management literature that I found helpful.

Then someone suggested I talk to John Davis, a business professor who has been studying family companies for years. He gave me the first breakthrough: a conceptual framework for understanding governance. The key is that people play multiple roles in a family business. At Ahlstrom, the cast of characters includes managers, board members, and family members. Some people play all three roles at once. Others are owners only. Sorting out the different perspectives inherent in these roles and relationships can really help you make sense of the dynamics of any issue or decision. (See "A Model of Family Business" at the end of this article.)

*How did you use this framework?*

Beyond the usual obstacles to communication, the emotions of family members tend to complicate an understanding of these roles. Whenever you have something you own in common, something that you care about—whether it's a company or a summerhouse—there will be great tension over disagreements.

The model helped us assess what was going on. We asked, How do the family, the board, and the business interact? And how *should* they interact? We began to see that those relationships would need to change over time, that we should expect them to be different in each successive generation.

*Why is that?*

In the first generation, the ownership and the management of the company are wrapped up in one person: the founder. In the second and third generations, a gap forms and gradually widens. Owners become more removed; they are less able to see what's happening to the business. But still they retain control. As that gap between owner and manager widens, it is critical that the business be run on professional terms, not on family terms. While that distinction may sound self-evident, it is rarely obvious to family members—and our family did not recognize it. Because we didn't understand the distinction, we had problems of trust. Keep in mind that it is often difficult for family members to sell their shares. So what happens if I am a family member, and I do not trust management or the board, and I cannot sell my shares? I am likely to make trouble.

***What kind of trust are you talking about?***

If the family is removed from the business, then trust means blind trust. And sometimes trust is undermined by people who want to gain something out of chaos. No family, when you really scratch the surface of it, is completely idyllic.

The kind of trust I'm talking about is based on information and knowledge. Public companies don't confront this issue in the same way because people are free to vote with their feet, by selling their shares. And public shareholders trust for various reasons. You trust GE for a different reason than you trust some other company.

***So you needed some mechanism to keep the family better informed?***

Yes—but more than that, we needed some way to bring the family together so that its 200 members could function in an organized way as *owners*. Working with some spirited members of the fifth generation, we developed two new institutions. The Family Assembly is one. The assembly consists of family members involved in owning the company as well as their spouses. It is more informal than the annual shareholders' meeting—big shareholders and small shareholders sit side by side. There were about 50 people at the last assembly. It's more of a social event than the annual shareholders' meeting, but it also serves as a forum for family members to discuss anything that's bothering them. A question might be asked about a specific business issue, such as why the company is going after a proposed acquisition in France. Or one might be asked about family involvement in, say, setting policy on composition of the board. We do have purely social meetings of the family, but they are occasions for people to get to know one another rather than to discuss business issues.

***"We needed some way to bring the family together so that its 200 members could function in an organized way as owners."***

The second institution we created is the Family Council. The council consists of five members elected by the Family Assembly. It serves both as a formal communication link between the family, the board, and the CEO, and as an informal sounding board for the CEO and the board. In addition, it prepares the assembly meetings, drafts family position papers, and suggests candidates for board membership.

***What kinds of issues does the Family Council consider?***

One issue they tackled early was the important question of what the family wants from the company. An obvious answer is that the family wants dividends. But it's critical for the family as owners to come to a common understanding of what that means. Do you want dividends that are steady, but low, so that people can plan their personal finances into the future? Or do you want the dividends to fluctuate with the company's results?

Another issue the council took up early on was the company's ethical values. We want Ahlstrom to be very ethical in its dealings with customers and employees. But what are the values of the family? Should we have rules, for example, regarding family members working inside the company?

***How is an issue like that resolved?***

Initially, there's a discussion. In this case, some people thought that anybody with ownership should be given an opportunity to work in the company. But others said, "Well, wait a minute. I don't want some unqualified manager destroying my capital just because he's a relative." The resolution to that particular question was simple: only qualifications count.

Now, when I say that is how it was resolved, understand that you don't vote on an issue like that. Over time, consensus has to emerge from the council's discussion.

***How do you make sure that everyone accepts the consensus view?***

Because there are 200 of us—and the family is growing—we had to put our values and practices in writing. The Family Council drafted a document—the Ahlström Family Values and Policies—that was extensively discussed. The discussion and the final document that emerged were an enormous help in bringing the family to a common view of its relationship to the company.

### *What does the document do?*

It functions like a constitution. At one level, it spells out the rights and responsibilities of ownership. In drafting and discussing the document, we were all reminded of a powerful reality that families forget easily—namely, that the company is of great importance to us all, both socially and financially. Thus it is in our interest to come together as responsible owners to ensure the company's future success. The statement of family values was a way of underscoring the basic principles that needed to be reinforced among the owners.

Beyond that, the document provides broad guidance from the family on what kind of company we want to be, setting boundaries for the company's strategy. We define ourselves as an industrial company in technology-driven fields. That's what we know best, and we want to stick to that definition.

The document also lays out our governance mechanisms. It describes the family institutions—the assembly and the council—and specifies the composition of the board and the qualifications for board membership. In addition, it addresses a handful of critical policies on such matters as dividends and CEO succession.

Today, as we move into the fifth generation, the role of the family is to own but not to manage the company. The family's ownership, however, is not passive. The family has decided that its role is to be an enlightened owner.

### *How do you define enlightened ownership?*

To answer that question, I need to put it in context. Family-owned companies that manage to survive into the third generation are vulnerable to the complacency of their owners. By then, the family takes for granted that the company will always be there to support them. They've been pampered and sent to the best schools. It's natural to think the business was handed to them by the gods and they are just along for the ride. So the third generation is likely to miss fundamental changes in the environment that require the company to adapt or rethink its original business logic.

***"We have a saying in Europe. It translates as The first generation creates, the second inherits, and the third destroys."***

The death rate for companies at this stage is so high that we have a saying for it in Europe. It translates as The first generation creates, the second inherits, and the third destroys. In German, it is a wonderful play on words: *Erwerben—vererben—verderben.*

***In English we have a similar saying: From rags to riches to rags in three generations. As a member of the fourth generation, then, your job was to restore the company?***

Yes. The fourth generation often has to make drastic changes, and that was the case in our company. It's unusual for family companies to survive into the fourth generation and beyond. The oldest family companies I know—I know of some that have lived through seven generations, for example—are usually connected to a stable business that depends on very focused expertise and location, such as wine making. But in most industries, where the business logic changes over time, family businesses often fail to adapt successfully. So usually by the fourth generation, professionalizing the management of the company is absolutely critical.

***Tell us how you fostered enlightened ownership.***

In 1995, with the help of Alden Lank and Fred Neubauer, two professors from IMD, and our personnel department, we inaugurated formal training aimed at family members in their twenties and thirties. For each participant, we held a series of three workshops, each lasting two very full days.

We tried to teach this younger generation what it means to be an owner. What happens inside the company? How is strategy formulated? What is personnel management? How are the company's values put into practice? How does the company budget its resources? What accounting principles does an owner need to master? What questions should an owner ask?

The professors used case studies as well as seminars. Everyone was brought into the discussion. Many of the family members are either just starting business careers or working outside industry—in archaeology or music or whatever. The most striking reaction among the students was their surprise at how complex the modern corporation is.

***Were you personally involved in those training sessions?***

Yes. I and other managers from the company made presentations. It was fascinating to have my own children and my nieces and nephews as students. More important, the sessions gave me the opportunity to understand the younger people's mood, something the leader of a family business needs to do. One part of leading is testing the waters. Another part is creating a shared vision by reacting and responding to the family's general mood. Enlightened owners must have a shared vision of where the company is headed. They don't need a lot of data or an analytical understanding of every strategic issue. It's more a question of how they feel about the company in their hearts—or in the pits of their stomachs.

When starting the sessions, we first asked everyone to draw a picture—the way children do in kindergarten—showing what kind of company Ahlstrom is. They drew their pictures and glued collages and then had some fun analyzing them. And when they had finished, I said, "Now I would like you to tell me what kind of company you want Ahlstrom to be in the future?" And then I showed them three pictures.

The first showed a small toy boat in a pond with a boy looking on. I asked them whether they'd like the company to be that kind of boat. The second was a drawing of an old-fashioned junk sailing in Hong Kong harbor, with the skyline in the background. I asked, "Would you like it to be this junk, steadily sailing by the modern world but not really part of it?" And then I showed them a picture of a high-tech ocean racer sailing on the edge of Niagara Falls. It's a scary picture, in fact. It's clear that the boat is winning against the falls, but it's dangerous.

And I asked them, "Which of these boats would you like to be? Are you comfortable projecting yourself into that high-tech boat doing dangerous things? Or would you be happier with something slower and safer that you can control?"

***It's hard to imagine the CEO of a public corporation asking such questions of shareholders. Do you think this dimension of leadership is unique to family enterprises?***

Yes. The leaders of the family—whether that means the CEO, the chairman of the board, or any other family member—have to try to keep everybody reasonably happy. I doubt that Jack Welch needs to ask his shareholders such questions. Warren Buffett might ask them, but he's a very unusual person. For Ahlstrom, however, it is vital to keep family members interested and on board.

***As you prepare the younger generation of the family to be enlightened owners, are you also on the lookout for managerial talent? Do you make any special effort to recruit people from the family who have the right skills?***

It's not a bad thing to be a family member and work in the company, but what you find in a family company is that family members are treated with an extra degree of respect. If they make a mistake, it is somehow covered up by the organization around them because nobody wants to confront a family member and say, "Well, you goofed it. You goofed." They never want to say that.

So it is difficult for a family member to learn the ropes inside the company. And that is why I say, "Prove your salt elsewhere first so that I can be sure that you have learned, really learned, to take criticism and to stand for your own mistakes."

***So even if there were people in the family you felt had great potential as managers, you would advise them to work at other companies first, for their own sake as well as for the sake of the business?***

Particularly for their own sake.

***That's an interesting point. Is there a similar problem in trying to attract top-management talent to the company? That is, will people from outside feel they might***

***not have the same opportunity as a family member to advance?***

I hope not. I don't think any good family-owned corporation can afford to get only the second best. Our company has a good reputation. Whenever there's an opening, we always have a flood of applications. But it's conceivable. I often hear that if you need good people in southeast Asia, it pays to look in the family-owned overseas Chinese companies, where disgruntled people believe they will not get the same career opportunities as family members.

***"Succession creates enormous tension. Who will carry on the company's legacy?"***

But we take seriously the idea that competence is more important than family ties when it comes to running the business. My successor, who was appointed by the board, is not a family member.

***CEO succession is one of the most difficult issues for family companies. It is often in the handoff between generations that family companies fail. As you tackled the broader question of governance at Ahlstrom, how did you approach succession?***

In the early 1990s, we asked Lank and Neubauer of IMD to do a study with us of the state of governance in family companies. Because so little has been published on the subject, we had to do our own field research, interviewing the heads of a number of family-owned businesses of our size, mostly in Europe, some in the United States. We asked the family leaders what problems they faced and how they had solved them. Most had struggled with a common set of governance issues, but two seemed especially important for us. We have already discussed one: the relationship between the family and the business. The second was succession: how the company chooses the next leader. Succession creates enormous tension. It can be a terrible headache. Who will carry on the company's legacy?

With my interest in history, I could see that our problems were exactly the same as those faced by the minikingdoms of Renaissance Europe. Fortunately, modern companies have found far less bloody ways to resolve succession than was the case in, say, fifteenth-century Italy. So our problem was by no means unique.

Once we understood that we had to separate the roles of family, ownership, and management, the solution was very straightforward: we had to choose the CEO based on competence alone. And that's what the board did. If the CEO is not a family member, as in this case, so be it. When that happens, the family has indicated in the policy document that it is desirable to select a family member to be chairman of the board.

***That sounds straightforward. But how do you ensure the same level of competence for the board that chooses the CEO?***

We spent a lot of time and effort on the question of board effectiveness. The level of professionalism on the board is frequently a problem in family companies. I felt it was extremely important to have a value-adding board.

Most people think the board exists to control the company. No. It does much more. It adds value. It should bring other viewpoints to management's attention. It does more than ask difficult questions, which is what all weak board members say they do. Nonsense. Anyone can ask difficult questions. But to ask questions that shed new light on an issue—that's really valuable, because it leads to the best possible solutions.

After decades of shareholder dominance on the Ahlstrom board, there was some resistance to bringing in professional outsiders. But then I asked, "If you are seriously ill, would you go to your relative who happens to be a not-so-good country doctor or would you go to the best specialist in the country?" And the answer was obvious.

We did something very unusual. We had the board members evaluate their own competence in adding value. Then the results were compiled, and the chairman was given the results so that he could act on them.

The upshot of our work on the effectiveness of the board was a change in the composition of Ahlstrom's main board. Today we have better balance, having added three experienced CEOs from major companies and two deputies from the fifth generation to the group of four family members and one family friend.

***Can you explain your reference to the main board? Are there other boards?***

Yes. We have organized the company to allow each of our four business groups to operate autonomously under an industrial holding company. (See the chart "From Sectors to Business Groups.") Each of those groups has its own CEO and its own board. Given the skills of the fifth generation, which are not in manufacturing, the holding-company structure with professional boards for each business group was the best fit.

The Ahlstrom Corporation had a long journey as it moved from being a very diversified company to being a

*From Sectors to Business Groups*

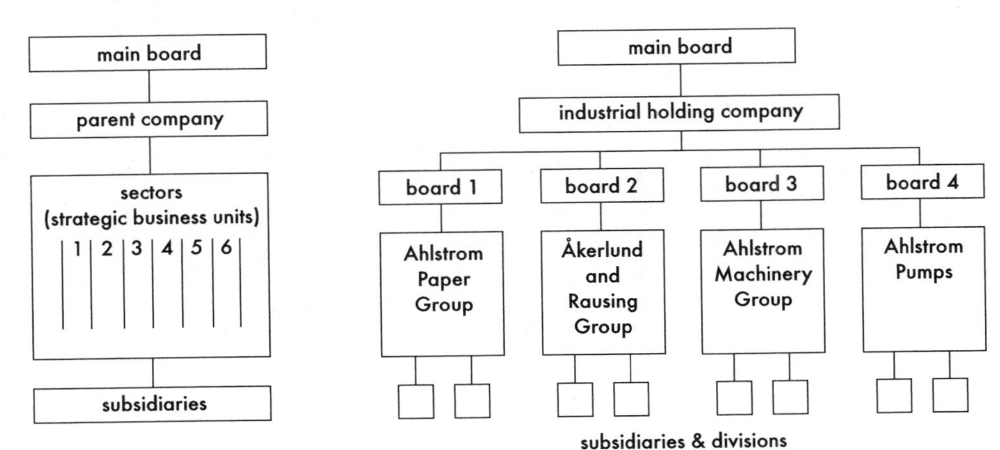

more focused company. Had we been publicly owned, I would have said, "Let's focus on only one business and let the shareholders spread their risks by investing in other things." As a family, we needed to spread our risk by being in three or four businesses.

***As you move to the fifth generation, it's clear that you continue to believe that Ahlstrom should remain a family-owned enterprise. Why is that?***

The materialistic answer is that a fortune is better managed if you keep it together. Split it into 200 parts, and it is unlikely to be managed as efficiently. We think we can do better than a mutual fund.

But there are also intangibles like the respect that comes from being part of a great industrial family. I know families that have been forced to sell their companies, and they are shocked by the loss of status that follows. And there's a sort of cohesiveness. Family members have a feeling that they belong somewhere. Although there might be some fighting in the family, there's also a good deal of support.

And there is this feeling that we are carrying on a great tradition. Usually families put up with a lot of hardship to see their companies survive. Most find it very hard to give up because they think, This has been handed down to me by my forefathers, and I'm supposed to take care of it. What drives most family companies to sell out is not a lack of interest among family members but rather an inability to resolve some difficulty—fighting within the family or poor profitability, for example. By then, the company is often in deep distress. In fact, it's probably too late.

There's huge potential in family companies today that is being wasted. In Europe, family companies have come under attack from the left, which opposes the inheritance of wealth. Some people do not realize how strong a driving force caring for one's children can be. And if you deny that force, you destroy a lot of value.

To avoid such controversy, family companies often go out of their way to keep a low profile. As a result, they have not been able to learn from one another. I'd very much like to see that change.

***You've been the head of the Ahlstrom Corporation for 15 years. Does that make you, by definition, the leader of the family?***

In most families, it's probably better not to be too explicit about that question. The families I know do not appoint family leaders. Historically, benign leaders have not appointed themselves. I don't think Winston Churchill ever said publicly that he was the leader of Great Britain during the Second World War. On the contrary, he said, "It was Parliament. I just provided the roar."

The changes we've been through at Ahlstrom over the past 15 years have taught me some lessons about leadership in a family business, and especially about the pacing of change. When it comes to strategic change, you have to be careful because you can't make too many mistakes. But once you have made your decision, you must be very, very fast in implementing it. With governance, you must be patient because you cannot change the way people think overnight. And finally, when it comes to the family—because there is so much emotion involved—you must be even more patient.

## Ahlstrom's Roots

### *by Krister Ahlström*

MY GREAT-GRANDFATHER Antti Ahlström founded the company in 1851. He was a farmer's son who started out in a very small way in shipping–from the west coast of Finland to various ports in the Baltic. He was successful and gradually bought bigger and bigger ships. By 1890, he had one of the largest shipping fleets in Finland, and his boats sailed to the Mediterranean and as far as Burma and Singapore.

At that time, a lot of old ironworks in Finland were going bankrupt because they had not kept up with technology. The ironworks needed charcoal, and so they were sited on vast forests. Because Antti Ahlström engaged in all kinds of trade as a shipper, he understood that the forests were ultimately more valuable than the ironworks. He put his knowledge to practical use, buying certain ironworks and forests very cheaply. He realized he could make a lot of money by converting the ironworks into sawmills. By 1900, Ahlstrom had the largest sawmills in all of Scandinavia.

Antti died just before the turn of the century, and his young son took over. Walter Ahlström was something of a gambler, and he set out with an ambitious plan. He bought two important industrial companies, Warkaus and Karhula, for which he paid far too much. He financed those acquisitions through debt notes.

The First World War came, bringing terrible inflation along with it. What otherwise would have been a foolish gamble turned into a stroke of genius. Once the war ended, the debt was easily repaid with inflated currency. And Walter had the plants. Of course, he never saw what he had done as a gamble. To him, it was a very sound business decision.

---

## A Model of Family Business

THE THREE-CIRCLE MODEL of family business is a useful tool for understanding the source of conflicts and priorities in family-owned enterprises. Originally developed in 1982 by John Davis and Renato Tagiuri, the model describes how any individual can be linked to the business: as a family member, an owner, and an employee. And because the circles overlap, anyone can fit into one, two, or three of these roles at once.

The model clarifies the special tensions that often crop up in family businesses. A person in sector 4, for example—a stock-owning family member who is not an employee—might argue that the company should be paying higher dividends. He might be at odds with someone in sector 7—a company vice-president who also happens to be his sister. She wants to reinvest in the company's expansion, which would improve its long-term outlook. The model can help the leaders of family businesses resolve such differences by sorting out the personal from the professional.

The model is not a one-size-fits-all framework. In the Ahlstrom Corporation's case, it was modified to reflect the company's dynamics. Thus the three circles were labeled as the family (left circle), the board of directors (top), and top management (right).

How can the model be applied? Consider the company's debate over selling the paper mill. On one side, there was strong opposition from sector 4: family and board members. The mill, after all, was synonymous with the family name. It took someone from sector 6–Krister Ahlström, a family member who was also the CEO but not yet on the board–to separate the emotional attachment to the mill from the business need to strengthen the company as a whole for the future.

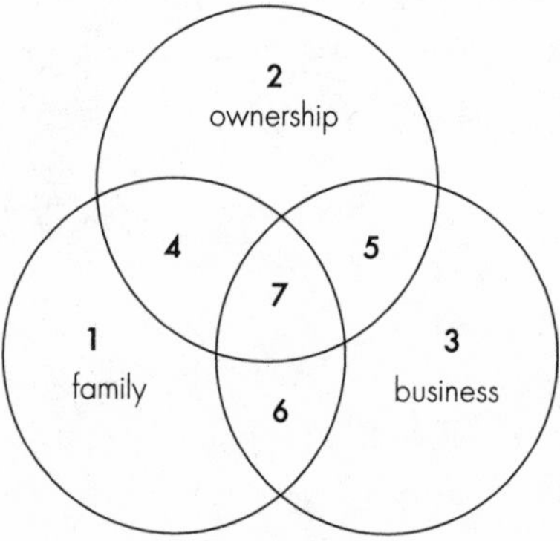


*The version of the three-circle model pictured here can be found in* Generation to Generation: Life Cycles of the Family Business, *by Kelin E. Gersick, John A. Davis, Marion McCollom Hampton, and Ivan Lansberg (Harvard Business School Press, 1997).*

**Originally published in January–February 1998**
**Reprint 98107**

# Common Sense and Conflict

## *An Interview with Disney's Michael Eisner*

SUZY WETLAUFER

## Executive Summary

ONCE UPON A TIME, the Walt Disney Company was famous for a quaint little mouse, a collection of vintage animated films for children, and two enjoyable–but aging–theme parks. It was, in other words, a great American company in eclipse.

Today, Disney may be going through some tough times, but it's tough times for a vast $23 billion empire. Along with animation blockbusters like *The Lion King* and *Beauty and the Beast,* Disney now owns three motion picture studios, as well as the ABC and ESPN television networks. The company is now poised to build new theme parks in Japan and China to go along with its EuroDisney attractions. Two Disney cruise ships sail the Bahamas. A Disney symphony to mark the millennium opened at the New York Philharmonic last fall. And an integrated network of Web sites–Disney.com, ABC.com,

ABCNews.com, Go.com, and Family.com–stretches out over the Internet.

The driving force behind all that growth was undoubtedly Michael Eisner, who became chairman and CEO in 1984. In this interview with senior editor Suzy Wetlaufer, Eisner vividly and colorfully describes the challenges he confronted as he built Disney. In a series of revealing anecdotes, he illustrates the workings of a culture that fosters creativity–an environment fraught with both carefully institutionalized conflict and good old-fashioned common sense.

Eisner describes in detail the four pillars of his particular brand of leadership, which he maintains are the same in good times and bad: being an example; being there; being a nudge; and being, as he puts it, "an idea generator–all the time, all day, all night."

---

*Once upon a time, the Walt Disney Company was famous for a quaint little mouse, a collection of vintage animated films for children–including* Fantasia *and the beautifully antique* Snow White and the Seven Dwarfs*–and two enjoyable but aging theme parks. It was, in other words, a great American company in eclipse.*

*Today, the sun never sets on the Disney entertainment empire. Along with its animation business, creator of blockbusters such as* Beauty and the Beast *and* The Lion King*, Disney now owns three other studios–the solidly commercial Touchstone Pictures and Hollywood Pictures, and the brainy, independent Miramax Film Corporation, maker of* Shakespeare in Love*. The company has brought its U.S. theme parks to new heights–literally and figuratively–and, after a bumpy start, has successfully exported the park business to Japan and*

*France. Two new Disney cruise ships,* Wonder *and* Magic, *sail the Bahamas; 725 Disney stores populate malls around the world; a Disney re-creation of the African savanna, Animal Kingdom, opened to rave reviews in Florida two years ago; and a Disney symphony to mark the millennium opened at the New York Philharmonic last fall. Disney's California Adventure is under construction in Anaheim and so is DisneySea in Tokyo. Now it appears that Disney will build a park in Hong Kong as well. Last, but certainly not least, Disney's acquisition campaign of recent years has brought on board a heap of media properties, including ABC, the sports cable network ESPN, Lifetime, E! Entertainment Television, and the Internet portal Go.com. Put it all together, and the company, with $23 billion in revenues, has become, in the words of one Wall Street analyst, "the mouse that roared."*

*Inarguably, the driving force behind Disney's metamorphosis has been Michael Eisner, who became CEO and chairman in 1984 after a brief and intense battle for the job. Eisner was desperate to run the floundering studio, but some of its board members had to be convinced that he had the requisite business sense. Indeed, at the time, Eisner was known mainly as a creative genius. In the 1970s, as head of programming, he turned around a moribund ABC with a plethora of hit shows, including the soap opera* One Life to Live; *the sitcoms* Happy Days *and* Welcome Back, Kotter; *and the critically acclaimed miniseries* Rich Man, Poor Man *and* Roots. *In the 1980s, Eisner rebuilt Paramount Pictures into a Hollywood powerhouse with a long series of commercial hits, including* Saturday Night Fever *and* Raiders of the Lost Ark. *Still, as Eisner stepped into the top spot at Disney, no one was really sure he had the right stuff to translate great ideas into top-line growth and bottom-line profitability.*

*He did. Disney's performance may currently be soft, but its long-term record is strong–20% annual earnings growth for 14 consecutive years and an annualized ROE of 18.5%–and some industry watchers think it is just a matter of time before Disney rebounds. (For more on Disney's current performance, see "We'll Be Right Back" at the end of this article.) As you'd expect, Eisner himself is optimistic, and in this interview he explains why. Disney, he says, is a company built on a powerful combination of institutionalized creative friction–an environment that produces a constant stream of ideas–and good, old-fashioned common sense–which "edits" those ideas for broad commercial appeal. Together, he says, conflict and common sense yield creativity. And in business–no matter what business–creativity "has a way of cleaning up the balance sheet and making the income statement shine very brightly."*

*In this interview, conducted at ABC headquarters in New York, the 57-year-old Eisner also discusses several other managerial challenges he has confronted and in most cases overcome while at Disney's helm. He describes what he calls the four requirements of leadership: being an example, being there, being a nudge, and being–as he puts it–"an idea generator, all the time, day and night." How else, he asks, can you keep reinventing a company?*

---

***Disney comes out with at least two products a week, from new rides at the theme parks, to TV shows and***

***movies, to CD-ROMs, to Little Mermaid makeup kits. How does all that innovation happen?***

This whole business starts with ideas, and we're convinced that ideas come out of an environment of supportive conflict, which is synonymous with appropriate friction. We create a very loose environment where people are not afraid to speak their minds or be irreverent. They say what they think, and they are urged to advocate strongly for ideas. That can be very noisy. It can be hard, too, because when you're loose, you say a lot of things, you challenge, you cajole, you provoke. Uninhibited discussion gets ideas out there so that we can look at them and make them better or just get rid of them if they don't work.

***How do you create the environment for supportive conflict?***

A bunch of ways. First, there's the culture. We like to think we have fun here. We laugh a lot. We're loosey-goosey.

I started my career as an usher at NBC, which had a very heavy atmosphere of reverence. The ushers had to memorize the names of all the executives, and when they came in, you greeted them in a very formal way. Then I worked for a year and a half at CBS, where everything was also very serious and conservative. Everybody wore very nice advertising-agency suits. And I thought, "Is this what business really is? Am I back in prep school?"

Finally, I found ABC, quite by accident, at a time when it was really struggling. People used to say, "Hey, put the Vietnam War on ABC; it will be over in 13 weeks." I was at a rather low level in the company in the beginning, but I saw how the executives got through the bad times—the same way I imagined doctors do in wartime—with humor, perhaps even gallows humor at some points. Even though times were hard, work was fun and exciting, and so I've taken that as part of my management style. I mean, we weren't curing cancer during my career at ABC, or during my eight years at Paramount, and we are not curing cancer at Disney. We're entertaining people, so we should have an energized culture. Maybe we don't whistle while we work, but we do smile and tell jokes.

Of course, that kind of culture doesn't just happen—you have to make it happen. That's one of the reasons we started doing our own internal "gong show" back in the 1970s. We started it at ABC, then it went to Paramount with me, and it's still at Disney, in some divisions. It started as a concept where, once a week, we'd invite everybody to come to a conference room, and anyone could offer up an idea or two and, right on the spot, people would react. We loved the idea of big, unruly, disruptive meetings; that's what the gong show was all about. *The Little Mermaid* came out of a gong show, and so did *Pocahontas*. Lots of ideas came out of those meetings, and people had a great time. Gong shows still go on in the animation business, but they've sort of faded off in other parts of the company. That's part of getting big and successful. Suddenly, very, very important people don't want to put themselves into the position of getting "gonged." Not everybody likes having his or her idea dismissed.

Another way we get creative juices going and ideas flowing is with "charettes." These are meetings with our architects and theme park designers. I love them because they are so brutally honest. Because everybody has a different opinion about color and style and size and look and landscaping and all the rest, these meetings take on event stature. Eventually resolution arrives, but not before every possible idea is put on the table.

Developing a movie or television show is a little different. I grew up at Paramount, and then in my early years at Disney, putting everybody in the same room for ten or 12 hours. Or it could be two days. The longer, the better. The more excruciating, the better. The first several hours can be a complete waste of time. The younger executives want to impress the older executives. The shy executives want to be shy. The loquacious executives dominate the room. Nothing happens. Eventually everybody gets hungry, and tired, and angry, and eager to leave.

But everybody also becomes equal. There is no pecking order. All of a sudden it gets really creative. You may have a ten-hour meeting, but it's during the last half hour that the best ideas come out. Everybody starts driving each other crazy with ideas, and then somebody says something and it all comes together.

***So there has to be a certain letdown of pretense before the creativity flows?***

Basically, yes. And you get that when you've been in the same clothes, in the same room, with the same turkey sandwiches getting dry in the same corner for a long time. I'm told even the Beatles had to play and play and play before they found their real creativity, their own style. Back in the early 1960s, even before they had Ringo Starr, when Pete Best was on drums, they would go to Hamburg, Germany, to make a living at little waterfront bars, and they would play every day, 18 hours straight to exhaustion. They were the C act at a lot of little places. They started out imitating Elvis; then they'd imitate someone else and someone else. Eventually, they were so exhausted, they couldn't copy anyone else, and they became themselves. They became the Beatles. Sometimes you have to be worn out and burnt out to become authentic and original.

So, our long meetings—our charettes and gong shows and movie development meetings—they're like playing music at a crummy little bar for 18 hours. It's a way to force ideas out and then edit them. Because essentially we're editors in this business. The executives and managers at creative companies are editors of other people's work. In fact, we consider that our job. We're editors of architects, we're editors of screenwriters, and we're editors of sports shows. We don't just come up with ideas. We listen to other people's ideas, and we tweak them, change them, refine them, and hopefully improve them.

By the way, the creative process doesn't stop when we talk about strategy or finance. Our culture of supportive conflict has become institutionalized. When we sit in business meetings, we stay and talk and talk until we figure out how to increase cash flow, or reduce corporate duplication, or rethink our hurdle rates. It may not be as much fun as the creative process around movies or TV shows, but it works.

***Are there any other ways that Disney institutionalizes an environment for creativity?***

Diversity is a great force toward creativity. For many, many years, we have made a huge effort to make our cast members, as we call our employees, a diverse group of people. We don't believe in a diverse workforce to mirror society solely because it's right. We also believe in diversity because the more diverse you are as an organization, the more diverse are the opinions that get expressed, which sometimes creates friction, and friction slows down the machine. When the machine slows down, good things can happen. If it is just sliding along with no friction, you get the easy solution; you get mediocrity. We work very hard on getting diversity at the top of the organization, and like many organizations we still have room to improve. That will make us more creative.

And I'm not just talking about diversity in skin color or ethnic background. I'm talking about diversity in point of view. That's why, as a company, we encourage individualism more than any place I know. We want people who work here to look at the world differently from one another. They can be white, they can be African-American, they can be Indian or Chinese or Latino—it doesn't really matter. The important thing is that they look at the same problem and bring their own individuality to the solution.

***Do costs ever come into the creative process? Should they?***

Absolutely. We are always looking for creative solutions to problems—and solutions that cost less money. Remember we still run a business; art and commerce go together. I often quote Woody Allen saying, "If show business wasn't a business, it would be called show show." Everything we do must not only be creatively responsible but also fiscally responsible, whether we're talking about an acquisition or a corporate financing or a scene in a movie. And in the end, the most creative and sound solutions will emerge. Finding a solution is, by definition, a creative act.

Here's an example from one of the first movies our team made at Disney. It was called *Outrageous Fortune*. The script called for a scene in an apartment where the main character, played by Shelley Long, asks her parents for money to go to ballet school. The entire movie was too expensive, and here was a scene that could be cut. Of course, the writer wasn't crazy about that idea, so suffice it to say, there was conflict over how to bring down the budget, and there was friction over this scene. People disagreeing.

But from those conversations came the idea that the scene could be played with Shelley Long making her request into the intercom in front of her parents' apartment building. No sets. No additional actors. She's basically begging them through a little phone buzzer in an already-built exterior set. And when she's done, you see this check floating down into the scene. That's all. It cost about $1.82 to make. And you know what? The scene was so much better and so much funnier than what the script originally called for because somebody had a different point of view about how it could be done. There was a nice resolution of conflict that made sense in terms of creativity and cost.

Another boost to creativity and cost can be delay. Sometimes an instant "I love it. Let's go make it now" response is appropriate. But more often, some delay helps. Now, we've been accused of not giving quick answers. And if a manager is not giving answers because he is on the golf course, then he should go work on his putting and forget the entertainment business. But if delay is a tactic to test someone's passion for an idea, to incubate it, whether it be an actor or a director or another executive, then delay is good.

Now, not everybody immediately understands the virtue of delay. At Paramount, there was a very eager and effective administrative executive who suggested to my boss that I be fired for not giving quick answers. This was a very organized guy who could move a wall six feet, if he was told which way to go, and he liked to move very fast.

One day, my boss called me to his office, and with this junior executive sitting there, my boss said, "Now, help me understand. We've won the Academy Award every other year for the last seven years. We've been number one in the box office for the last six years. We've got five of the top ten television shows. I think we've done a pretty good job. Why is it you want Michael Eisner fired?"

This was a very unpleasant moment for this executive, as you might imagine. But he answered. He said, "You don't give me answers. I ask you who we should have for a director on a picture, and you say, 'Let me think about it.' When I come to you guys with an idea, you don't jump up and say, 'Let's do it.' You're just too slow."

My answer to that was: "Sometimes in our business the best thing to do is nothing. Sometimes the best thing to do is delay—because it buys you two things. First, it buys you time to incubate an idea, to let it simmer in your brain so you can edit it yourself and improve on it. And the second thing it buys is the ability to see the truth. Because a delay lets you know how deeply someone believes in an idea. If a person really believes, he'll fight for it. He'll create a stink—friction, that is. And if he doesn't believe, he'll back off. And then you can negotiate for what you want—like another version of the idea or another director for the movie." And that was the end of the meeting.

So we like to build a bit of delay into the creative process at Disney. We don't go on impulse most of the time, and when we do, we chalk it up to inconsistency, which is also part of the creative process. Usually we talk about ideas. Some people think we talk them to death. But discipline is part of the creative process, contrary to popular belief.

***That's true. There is a popular notion that creative people are impulsive and individualistic to extremes. You're saying that's not so?***

Absolutely. Discipline is part of creativity. Painters have to use a canvas size that can fit on a wall. They have to use certain kinds of paint. You just can't go and splash stuff around.

Discipline is good for the creative process, and time limits are good. An infinite amount of time to do a project does not always make it creatively better. The image of an artist being temperamental and acting like a 16-month-old child is usually false. It's a cliché that we've helped perpetrate in the movie business. Artists are always depicted as crazies. But in reality, insane artists are rare. In fact, some of the most creative people I've ever met—Steven Spielberg, George Lucas, I.M. Pei, Frank Stella, and Frank Gehry, just to name a few—are the most organized, mature individuals you'll ever meet. Not many creative people have the urge to cut off an ear.

***If ideas are the magic in Disney's formula of success, what's the "practical" part of the equation?***

Common sense. Clear-eyed, hardheaded common sense. You can't have just ideas. You have to test them, too—subject them to a reality check.

People sometimes call it something like "business acumen" or "a market perspective." That's not exactly what I mean. Common sense comes out at that moment of yes or no, and it boils down to good judgment, which is the same at work and at home. Either you have it or you don't. It comes from how your parents raised you, your education, your talent, your character—whether your ego is under control. It depends on the clarity of your mind. Because when you make a smart decision at work, it very rarely is based solely on data and research and reports. Your education, your life's research, your experiences—they are all part of your core. Then common sense has to take over. It's the innate ability to stop, stand back, and ask, "Does this make sense? Will it work?"

Right now, for instance, Disney is considering making an epic love story wrapped up in the events surrounding Pearl Harbor. It's a great story, but it needs some common sense applied to it. Usually when executives read a script, their notes deal with story and character. But every single comment I've made on this script so far has been about common sense as it relates to budget. Movies are just costing too much now, and our movie team is trying to change that.

Here's an example. The script says, "*Exterior train station, dawn. Danny walks to one of the three revolving doors back into the station. He takes the one on the far right. As he passes through, he doesn't see Evelyn rushing through the door.*" So, it's a train station; it's 1939. So, I just said here in my note, "Hey, why not a *bus* station?" It will cost several million dollars less to film. This is a nothing little note. It won't change the company or its strategic direction forever after. But it is possible that with this bit of common sense—repeated 30 times in this script—we may make a less expensive but equally exciting picture. And who knows, it could be a very profitable movie for Disney, assuming it was a good idea in the first place.

Let me tell you, by the way, what common sense is not. It is not audience research. For some reason, a lot of people in the creative industries think that you should come up with lots of great ideas and then subject them to audience research. But most audience—or customer—research is useless. Exit research is fine, even helpful, and a good thing. Audiences are honest generally on what they have just seen, but prospective research is ridiculous. If you conducted interviews after the movie *Titanic* came out, everyone would have told you they wanted another movie about a love affair and a sinking ship. But common sense tells you that if you made another movie like that, everyone would say, "Not again!"

***How does practical magic apply to branding issues? After all, the Disney brand dictates some pretty strict boundaries.***

We insist on good taste, if that's what you're referring to by boundaries, but I don't think that has limited our creativity. Actually, our commitment to good taste has forced us to be more inventive. The high road is often harder but more rewarding creatively. Our brand is our greatest asset, and we handle it with extreme care.

We think of a brand like a pointillist painting, an idea that I first heard about in a conversation with Warren Buffett. Everything you do for your brand is a point on the canvas. An advertising campaign is one point, say. Each customer's experience is a point. The quality of a new CD-ROM is a point—an animated movie, a Broadway show, a new theme park, and so on. At the end of a decade, you can have hundreds and thousands of new, wonderful, pretty points, and they can create a beautiful brand picture. But if you've been sloppy with some of your points, you can have an atrophied, old-fashioned, muddled picture, and no one is going to want to hang it on their wall. A brand takes a long time to build, and a long time to destroy, and both happen as a result of lots and lots of small actions. If you want to be strong, each point along the way has to be as close to perfect as possible.

Every day, every one of us here makes brand decisions. We have to, because our brand is so valuable to us. What does our brand stand for? we ask. Do mothers love us, but kids think we're old-fashioned? Do kids love us, but mothers think we have lost our way? That kind of questioning is just life here. Most of the time, the decisions get taken care of automatically by people on the line. Whether it is the ESPN brand or the ABC brand or the Disney brand, they are proud of their brands and protect them. Sometimes, however, the very hard decisions about the Disney brand get pushed up to me.

***Is the primary role of Disney's leader, then, to guard the brand?***

That's not really a role. It's an underlying responsibility; it's always there. Just like your responsibility to guard the company's assets for the shareholders. But a leader, in my opinion, really has four roles. You've got to be an example. You've got to be there. You've got to be a nudge, which is another word for motivator, really. And you've got to show creative leadership—you have to be an idea generator, all the time, day and night.

***What does leading by example entail?***

Who we are as people matters as much as what we do.

The company watches senior management; the cast members look to us as role models. So each one of us should work very, very hard at living up to that. I myself am inquisitive all the time—that's an essential part of the creative process. In the middle of a meeting on financial performance, I may say, "My wife and I were in Disneyland Paris two weeks ago. Alice's Maze is just not exciting enough. What can we do?" They'll look at me like, "How did Alice's Maze get into this meeting? We were talking about return on equity." But what I am showing is that any and all questions are fair game. We are open with each other, we probe, we push, we think about our company as an interrelated whole, and the quality of Alice's Maze has a direct impact on ROE.

Leading by example also means showing a combination of enthusiasm and loyalty to the institution, and it certainly means demanding excellence in the organization. We need to constantly demonstrate what we care about—synergy, for example. (For more on how Disney achieves synergy, see "Making Sure One Hand Washes the Other" at the end of this article.)

***What about "being there"? Can you describe what that role involves?***

Sometimes you just have to be there with your people. You have to be in the same room with them, look them in the eyes, hear their voices. I'll tell you one thing. Most of the bad decisions I've made, I've made while teleconferencing. In creative companies, you have to be able to read body language—see the look in people's eyes when an idea is launched, see whether they fall asleep.

If you have an organization that is small enough, being there simply means having contact and exposure and being available. When the organization gets bigger, it is unbelievably frustrating to a leader that you can't be there for everyone. That's why you need a team of leaders running the organization, which is what we have. Our parks have a leader. Our movie and television business has a leader. Our Internet operations have a leader. ABC and ESPN have leaders. We have country managers. And what makes organizations great is the quality of that leadership spread across the top—not just at the very top.

What I do is focus on the 40 people I have an impact on every day. I'm very available to them. And then I try to get out there as much as possible. Our management team is always moving around all over the company, which is all over the country and all over the world. We walk the parks, the hotels, and the stores. The most fun is going into the hotel kitchens late at night. In the next weeks, many of us are meeting the performing cast of the Broadway musical of *Hunchback of Notre Dame* in Berlin, followed by the opening-night party of *Lion King* in London. Then I'll spend a day with our management team in the U.K.

I'm also using e-mail more to communicate with our whole cast—all 110,000 of them. Today I'm going to send something out about why we closed Walt Disney World for Hurricane Floyd. We've never closed the park before, and everyone wants to know why. They want to know what we did to protect our cast members and our guests down there. So I'll tell them. It's a great way to stay connected.

### *What does it mean to lead by being a nudge?*

By nudging I mean that I just don't forget things. I don't keep many notes, but once something is in my head, I can't get rid of it until I think it has been stuck into somebody else's head. I am constantly reminding people of ideas. I follow up and follow up because good ideas have a way of getting lost. They fall through the cracks, or they get mired in bureaucracy, and everyone is busy in their own orbit. So I nudge. Sometimes all that good ideas or good people need is an advocate who won't shut up.

***When was the last time you played the nudge role?***

I do it every day. I've been doing it forever. For instance, a few years ago, I was walking around Walt Disney World, midnight, by myself. I got to a pavilion that was being renovated. I figured I would climb over the barricade and see what was going on. I started walking around, and pretty fast a junior security officer came toward me with a flashlight.

I introduced myself. Luckily he had heard of me. So, we got talking, and he knew where all the plans were. He wasn't involved in the construction at all, but he knew all about it. He was interested. He cared. He went through every page of the plans with me. He knew everything, and he really was passionate and intelligent about the project. It was obvious to me that this guy was special.

The next day, I went back to my office, and I wrote a note to the people at the park, saying, "This fellow—I think his name was Lamont—is a star. I think you should promote him." I wrote a note or mentioned him to somebody every two weeks for a long time, and every time I would say, "What's happening with Lamont?"

***You were CEO when this happened?***

Yes.

***And you had to write note after note to get someone promoted?***

There were 20 people above him.

***What happened?***

I think he's doing great. He certainly would have done just fine without me. But maybe I was helpful. It's not as if someone else wouldn't have noticed him soon enough. I mean, I don't want you to think that everything in this company has my stamp on it. It does not. It couldn't even if I wanted it to. We are too big, and we have too many amazingly creative people. I try to set an agenda, but I am still just a temporary manager of a great institution.

***The story about Lamont suggests that being a nudge takes endurance.***

Yes, sometimes you have to nudge people for years, literally. A lot of projects, especially in this business, take a long time. *Beverly Hills Cop* took eight years to make at Paramount. Animal Kingdom was ten years in the making. Everybody has to just keep pushing, pushing. Our corporate team, actually, has become one big nudge. I like that until they nudge me. Then I understand how annoying it can be, but I do react. We all do.

The day we acquired ABC, I started nudging them about a big-money game show. We all agreed it was an idea whose time had come. So, four years of nudging, and now we have *Who Wants to Be a Millionaire?* It's a big hit for us. In fact, it may even make ABC number one in prime time. Now, I had nothing to do with the creative content of the show. In fact, I kept pushing for something like *The $64,000 Question.* But I had something to do with the maniacal advocacy the show happened to require. So nudging is a very annoying role to play, but critical.

***The last role of a leader, you say, is being an idea generator. Should good ideas come from the top?***

It's better if good ideas come from the top than bad ideas. But ideas can come from anywhere. The leader in a creative business should be creative. He or she should be spouting ideas all the time, just like everyone else. Many of us come up with ideas driving to work, walking around the house, watching our kids at sporting events, everywhere. It becomes addictive. Many of my ideas are simply bad, and, believe me, I am told so quickly. That kind of honesty in our team and in our culture must exist—a culture where your associates tell you that your last idea was all wet. I have no problem telling an associate that I hate his idea. So we must have an environment where criticism goes up as well as down. We all edit each other. Sometimes the ideas do make some sense, and we move forward with them.

***One of the ideas the company moved forward with was your concept for a symphony. How did you come up with it?***

I was with my wife at a performance of Mahler's *Symphony for a Thousand.* I read the program wrong—I thought it said the symphony was commissioned by an Austrian duke to celebrate the turn of the century. It actually wasn't, but it got me thinking—Disney should have a symphony. We don't have a classical department, but why not? So the next day, I went to the office, and I wrote the story for the symphony. It was a really bad version of *Rich Man, Poor Man,* spanning from Hiroshima to the year

2000. I started it with Hiroshima because I thought it needed to start with emotion. Then I handed the idea off to people who knew what they were doing. They changed the story; they fixed up the idea, thank God.

***Does it make sense for the CEO of a global conglomerate with tens of thousands of creative employees to be spending his time writing the stories for symphonies and coming up with the ideas for game shows?***

Very few ideas for the company now come from me, actually. But I'm in the weeds, yes. That's the way I lead. And I've been criticized for it. A little while ago, the *Wall Street Journal* wrote a long article about our Internet portal Go.com, and they went on at length about its problems. At the end of the article, they said, the biggest problem with Go.com is that Michael Eisner is too much in the weeds. And I thought, "If the product is having problems, *shouldn't* I be in the weeds?"

By the way, over the years, I have come to the realization that there is no right and wrong with leadership. There is no exact formula. The right style of leadership varies by industry, by person, by the people you are leading. It is unrealistic to think that one leader's way is necessarily the only way. But I've got my way, and I've been lucky so far. Right now we are regrouping after the first lull in our earnings in more than a decade the only way we know how—through creativity. We've got three new theme parks under construction, eight animated movies in the works, a full slate of live-action motion pictures, new shows for ABC, new ideas for ESPN—and on and on. And then there is the Internet. Our goal is to lead in this space because we know that soon it will be where entertainment in the home consolidates. Hopefully, our good ideas about the Internet will outnumber our bad ones. But the only way to make that happen is to remember what Babe Ruth said when he was asked how he kept hitting home runs: "I just keep my eye on the ball." We just have to keep up the practical magic.

And to tell you the truth, I don't know any other way to lead than how I do it. Of course, I've never really thought about it as "leadership." I just want to be a part of a great group of people that comes up with new ideas. That's fun. And with the fun goes responsibility—responsibility for protecting the past and responsibility for planning for the future. In a creative person, just as in a creative company, you have to have both, a creative outlook and one that embodies common sense, side by side, inseparable. If you don't, then you get neither art nor commerce.

---

## Making Sure One Hand Washes the Other

*It is hard enough to get people in different divisions to work together creatively in a small company; the challenge of doing so in a very large one was a recurring theme in HBR's conversations with Michael Eisner. Below, Eisner discusses how Disney manages—with amazing success—to create synergy among its many far-flung businesses. But he also acknowledges that other challenges of bigness are extremely tough to overcome, in particular "overdelegation"—the relentless, nonsensical pushing down of authority in the name of empowerment—and the all-too-common element of surprise.*

***You'd have to live in a cave to miss a new Disney movie coming out, what with the cross-promotions on TV, on the Web, at the theme parks, at the Disney***

***stores, and even at McDonald's, with little Disney characters tucked in with the burgers and fries. What goes on inside Disney to make the blitz happen on the outside?***

First and foremost, it's Disney Dimensions, which is a program we run two or three times a year for 25 senior people from every division of the company worldwide. So far, 300 people have gone through it. It's like synergy boot camp. The people go through eight days of meetings covering every aspect of the company. They spend four days in California: in Burbank at the company headquarters, in Glendale at Disney Imagineering, and in Anaheim at Disneyland. They play characters in the park. They hear how you cook 100,000 meals a day. They see how the beds are made at our hotels. Then they spend three hours at Disney Video. They do four hours at Interactive. They spend time with the legal department, with corporate finance. They spend time with human resources to understand the values of the company. They have presentations from every division–animation, television production, computer services, research and development, consumer licensing, theatrical movie distribution–everything. Then they come to New York and spend two days at ABC, ESPN, and all that. Then they go to Walt Disney World and review all our businesses there. They learn what it is like to work in 100-degree heat and 100% humidity, to clean bathrooms, cut hedges, check out guests, and soothe tired children. They start at 7:00 in the morning, and they work until 11:00 every night for eight straight days. There are no phone calls, and they're not allowed to do any "regular" business.

Believe me, everyone starts off dreading Disney Dimensions. We know that. But by the third day, they love it. By the end of the eighth day, they have totally bonded. They've learned to respect what tens of thousands of people do, and they've become close friends at the same time.

When they go back to their jobs, what happens is synergy, naturally. When you want the stores to promote Tarzan, instead of the head of animation for Tarzan calling me, and me calling the head of the Disney stores, what happens is the head of Tarzan calls the head of the stores directly.

Synergy happens at Disney because it should. Our products scream out for synergy. If we build a new attraction at a park, or build a new park altogether, or make a new animated movie, it very naturally is on the cover of our magazines around the world. It's on the Disney channels around the world explaining how it was made. It could be in a trailer playing around the world in front of another Disney movie. And of course it would be displayed in the windows in our 700-plus stores, again around the world. There may even be a hangtag on millions of pieces of consumer products worldwide. And Disney Records will promote the music. There is not a single part of Disney where the left hand can't wash the right.

Take ABC. It gives us tremendous opportunity for synergy. When we open a new park or animated film, there will be a special about it on ABC. There will be institutional promotions on *One Saturday Morning.* ABC Radio broadcasts what is new at Disney 24 hours a day. And on and on.

***Has it always worked as perfectly as you describe it?***

No, of course not. Synergy is hard; it takes pushing from the top. I remember trying to create synergy when I was at

Paramount—I wanted us to put the names of our new movies in the Gulf & Western pay envelopes every week. I figured it was free advertising to 100,000 people. The senior management at Gulf & Western was not interested, so it didn't happen. For synergy to happen, the CEO and senior management have to push for it constantly.

We're also trying to increase the amount of synergy in our global operations country by country. We've just reorganized our international organization into a hybrid type of structure, so the person running movies in Italy, for instance, not only reports to an executive in the movie division, as he or she did before, but also reports to a country head. That country head is responsible for synergy. Hopefully, this will duplicate what we do in Burbank every week.

***What aspect of running a large company is the most daunting?***

Without a doubt, it's dealing on a day-to-day basis with the human equation—that is, making sure our cast members are committed and motivated, and that their emotions are engaged in the right ways. We make movies about conflict, ambition, envy, jealousy. In our movies, we look at what happens when healthy ambition turns into blind ambition, when normal needs for power turn into dictatorial power, when the appropriate search for opportunity turns into opportunism.

That's in the movies. In the work place, we don't want to see the dark side of emotions if we can help it. We want ambition and power and opportunity to be under control. We want our top managers to be comfortable with themselves and to be an example for the entire workforce.

**When managers set an example of how to behave, does that allow more autonomy throughout the organization?**

In some cases, yes. I'm a big believer in initiative and responsibility at every level. A ride operator at a Disney park should be able to adjust policies to address a guest's problems no less than a vice president of a division should be able to make decisions about how to move the organization forward.

But there have to be limits to autonomy. Our goal for senior management is to delegate authority–*authority*, not autonomy–downward in the organization. Sometimes in large companies, too much gets delegated, especially now that empowerment is the rage. I just believe that those with the most experience should be given the most opportunity to handle really tough situations–situations that put a company or a division at risk.

I have had tremendous authority at every job I've ever had. I took it–because in the real world, most responsibility you take, you're not given. But I managed up as well as sideways and down. If I had a feeling that something was going to be more expensive, or was going over budget, or was going to put a project at risk, I told my boss and my boss's boss. I figured they had to have some talent. That's how they got to the top. There are not too many dumb bosses out there.

So autonomy has its place. Delegation has its place. But sometimes you have to push problems back up to the top. Otherwise, you just might bump into the biggest corporate problem of all.

**Which is?**

Surprise. I mean, surprise is part of business, you can't avoid it. Everyday, something you're not expecting happens. But if you can see it coming, you can at least plan for it. And then of course it is not a surprise, and you can use your common sense to find a solution. And in business, common sense goes a very long way.

---

## We'll Be Right Back

*According to recent financial results, the Disney magic isn't exactly dazzling at the moment. Eisner explains why—and why he thinks the company will shine again soon.*

No doubt about it, we're in a tough period right now. But there's also no doubt that our business is not endemically under siege. We still have the right formula, the right foundation. Disney really has practical magic figured out. Not that we get it perfect every time, but we come very, very close a lot of the time. You can go anywhere in the world and see that in action. Go visit the Animal Kingdom in Orlando or take one of our cruise ships to the Disney island, Castaway Cay. If you look at people's faces, you'll see that Disney still knows how to sweep people off their feet, out of their busy or stress-filled lives, and into experiences filled with wonder and excitement. We sell fun and—not to sound arrogant, really just to sound proud—we still do that better than anyone.

But, yes, our earnings and stock price have suffered recently. Part of the reason is that we're experiencing a trough in our home-video earnings due to our strategic decision to lengthen the release cycle for certain animated movie classics. At the same time, our library of classics is still tremendously valuable, and as DVD penetration grows and major titles come back on-line, I believe that value will once again be readily apparent in our earnings stream.

Earnings in our consumer products division have also suffered, due in part to a slowdown in our licensed-character merchandising. It is critical that we push ourselves to execute better, be more creative in our approach, and ensure that we keep our merchandise relevant. And finally, the Internet–Go.com, Disney.com, ESPN.com, Family.com, ABC.com, and ABCNews.com are all tremendous assets, but they also take great investment. We are confident that the confluence of the computer and the television is coming. We are confident that our customers will get their movies and entertainment and news and information from the Internet. The digital world is here, and ABC and Disney and ESPN and Go.com will be together providing such software. But to take our place in the future takes some investment now.

I think Disney is well positioned for the future. Thank God we purchased ABC and ESPN. That acquisition will keep us strong and help keep gatekeepers from diverting our products. If the investment community does not value our assets as highly as we do, we will have an opportunity to further invest in our own equity. After the bulls and the bears have fought it out, my vote would be a vote for ownership in assets like Disney.

**Originally published in January–February 2000**
**Reprint 00111**

# About the Contributors

ALICE HOWARD is an independent consultant based in Cambridge, Massachusetts. Formerly a Manager with Bain & Company, she founded her own practice, Vista Consulting, which serves both for-profit companies and nonprofit organizations. A graduate of the Harvard Business School and the Harvard Graduate School of Education, she has had a longstanding interest in the management and performance of charitable nonprofit organizations in the United States.

JOAN MAGRETTA is a consultant and writer based in Cambridge, Massachusetts. A former Partner at the management consulting firm of Bain & Company, she writes on a wide range of management topics for publications such as the *Harvard Business Review* and the *Wall Street Journal.* Her interview with Michael Dell, included in this collection, won the McKinsey Award for the best article published in HBR during 1998. Her current book, *Managing in the New Economy,* is a collection of HBR articles. She is the coauthor of *How Management Works and Why It Is Everyone's Business,* to be published in 2001.

STEVEN E. PROKESCH is Director of Idea and Editorial Development at The Boston Consulting Group. Prior to joining BCG in 1997, Mr. Prokesch was a Senior Editor at the *Harvard Business Review.* An award-winning journalist, he previously worked for 17 years as an editor and a reporter at the *New York Times*, *Business Week*, and United Press International.

**SUZY WETLAUFER** is the Senior Executive Editor of the *Harvard Business Review*, and a specialist in the area of leadership, teams, and organizational behavior. In addition to the interviews in this volume, she is the author or coauthor of a number of HBR articles, including, "The Ways CEOs Lead," "The Team That Wasn't," and "A Question of Character."

# Index